Ten Conversations with Albanians

Ten Conversations with Albanians
Copyright © Albana Shala 2017

English language editor: Bryony Mortimer
Design: Daniel Chavez

First published in English by Carabela Books
Amsterdam, The Netherlands

ISBN: 978-90-827058-0-5

Ten Conversations
with Albanians

Albana Shala

To Andrea

Why this book?

It is many years since I left Albania and yet I still feel Albanian. The similarity between my name and the name of my country only adds to the emotional charge it has for me, no matter that I live far away. The pact was sealed a long time ago. Because of my language, my habits, my family, my friendships, my memories and my name, I canot liberate myself from my homeland. I circle around it, gazing at it with nostalgia, even sadness. Every act of construction, maintenance or improvement in the country gives me joy. Every violent episode, every story I hear about crime and corruption makes me angry and sad.

While orbiting Albania, I make, unmake and remake a little Albanian world of my own. This little planet of mine is populated with the friends with whom I shared my childhood and youth. You will find some of their stories within the pages of this book. My friends may not be aware of how intensely they live with me, in this dimension. And maybe it is better this way, otherwise our hands would be crippled by nostalgia. It is better to imagine ourselves sitting at a table with a glass of wine at my home in Amsterdam, or imagine how we might undertake a journey together across the world, or how we might all once get together and celebrate life on the Adriatic coast.

When I was 18 years old I said to my parents: 'Leave me alone, this is my life!' They smiled and pulled even tighter the visible and invisible strings that tied me to them. And yet, they were also trying, perhaps in vain, to live their own lives, were they not?

Today my friends live their lives as free men and women, as mothers and fathers, some are even grandparents. Life connects us with many visible and invisible strings inside and outside Albania, but after all these years we are still friends because we have chosen to remain so. No obligation, no authority, no ideology or higher power connects us or drives us towards each other. We see each other not often, and some friends I meet very rarely. Thanks to the Internet we can exchange news and photos, we can share memories and impressions and, above all, we can try to share our present. The portraits in this book are contemporary portraits, but they are drawn with knowledge and experience gained before and after 1991, the year in which Albania, the last domino of the socialist camp in Europe, fell.

In parentheses, it would be interesting to compare our conversations of 25 years ago with those we have today. I remember that our talks and whispers of those days were permeated by a desire to change, to be free and different, as well as by indignation, sadness and fear. Even the walls had ears then as the communist dictatorship gasped its last breaths.

The idea for this book came with my realisation that without my friends, Albania would not have such a gravitational pull for me – I would not orbit it like a moon. It is they, my friends, who make my return home meaningful, it is they who make contemporary Albania my Albania, despite my distance from it. It is the people who tell their stories here, and many other friends who do not appear in this book, who keep my planetary system in balance.

This book, more than anything else, is a chronicle of the time in which Albanians are living. It is a description of what is happening around us and within us. It is an effort to rediscover each other as individuals and as a group of people who experienced life under a dictatorship and now live in a free and democratic society. It endeavours to describe how a few Albanians who lived through the transition experience the 21st century.

It is an effort to share something of Albania with those who are not Albanians, readers who would like to know about Albania and the Albanians, from their own perspective. What makes them happy? What bothers them? What moves them? Do they feel fulfilled and in harmony with the world? What do they value? What do they want to do with their lives? Putting together these accounts somehow gave me a feeling of completeness.

In his book Microcosmos, the Italian writer Claudio Magris refers to identity as 'also a horror, because it owes its existence to tracing a border and rebuffing whatever is on the other side.' I mention this because we Albanians were born and brought up in a very isolated place. Albanian identity was characterised by our lonely state of existence – the result of an absurd antagonistic rejection of everything that came from the world beyond our borders.

I am aware that my decision to tell the stories of ten friends is a very personal one. When I asked them to be part of this book, which would explore their real lives, my friends responded immediately with good will and seriousness. They are not famous personalities or important people, although a few of them are becoming public figures. Albania is a small country, and free souls and strong individuals always stand out in such a place. (I doubt if there are any educated Albanians today who have not been tempted into television, who have never published a poem or a story in a local newspaper.)

I did not want this book to be dominated by politicians or by the outstanding figures who we see daily on our TV screens, as they take decisions about the country, as they promote their economic or cultural policies, as they talk on our behalf in parliament. Notwithstanding my appreciation for these people, I wanted instead to document the lives and deeds of ordinary people, the ones you meet on the street, on the beach, in the queue, in the fitness club, at the airport, at the kindergarten. None of us pretends to represent a generation or a nation, but as my friends and I reflect on our own lives we can share with the interested reader thoughts about where we come from as a people, where we are now, where we are going to in the future. Even more so if we consider the thousands of invisible strings which link us to our isolated past, a life which resembled that of George Elliot's characters in Middlemarch: A Study of Provincial Life. In 1870, Elliot used the metaphor of a web to describe life in the province: 'society is a web and one cannot disentangle a strand without touching all the others.' And so it is with these stories.

The conversations documented here took place over a period of two years, mostly in Tirana, and then continued on the Internet.

Ischa Meijer, a Dutch journalist of the last century, well known for his mastery of the interview, once said that a good question puts every answer in the shadow. This has not been my purpose in this book. If there is a lack of depth or insufficient contrast in these portraits, it is firstly due to my inexperience as an interviewer, given the sensitivities around some of the subjects and, later, the style I chose to write in. I do not think our conversations have ended here; neither the questions nor the answers have been exhausted.

Meijer added: 'In fact, I do not like it during interviewing to have another person near me, who has even his own thoughts and who says things. I would prefer to tell him: Indeed, I am interviewing you, but you better stay home. I will answer on your behalf, sincerely, I assure you it will be all right (and a nice one [interview]!)'.

With this I would like to thank all my friends for their time, their trust, their willingness to reveal themselves and to be the centre of attention. You are not perfect and that is why you are so wonderful. Thank you!

Albina

> *I was the world in which I walked, and what I saw*
> *Or heard or felt came not but from myself;*
> *And there I found myself more truly and more strange.*
>   Wallace Stevens: *Tea at the Palaz of Hoon*

Albina entered my life quietly. She was a young woman from Vlora, broad-shouldered, like all those who have grown up by the sea. Albina studied English, and lived at her aunt's house at the top of Kavaja street in Tirana, not far from the Writers' League. Hotel California was later erected nearby, followed by a gas station, and finally a mosque. Today the mosque stands side by side together with the traditional Catholic and Orthodox churches, which once lay sole claim to the street.

Kavaja Street is my street and the street of many peers who lived and attended the elementary and secondary schools of that neighbourhood. In the yard of her aunt's house grew a white flower, 'sweet magnolia'. Each time I think about Albina, the magnolia and the garden of that house comes to my mind too. Its existence used to give our endless talks a degree of romanticism and harmony. I have shared with Albina a passion for literature, a love for the sea, a sense of humour and our dreams. Albina takes after her mother, Gjinofeva. She likes to speak, to laugh and to joke, never moralising, and above all she is an optimist, who finds an opportunity in everything. In those years, Albina represented to me the people of the coast, simply because I did not know much about that region of Albania.

The years went by and Albina was lucky to experience the political change in the country during the last year of her studies. Along with hundreds of fellow students, hungry and tired from the dogmas and the speeches, she protested, doing what students do everywhere – questioning the status quo. Who could protest and better mobilise others than she? Albania had killed the fear before the students' protests began.

Albina had fallen in love with George, one of the few foreigners who lived and worked in Albania at that time, an employee of the Greek Embassy in Tirana. She had shown courage, faith and a free spirit by not accepting to break up with him. And the pressure to do so was enormous.

In those days, every foreigner was considered a potential enemy, a spy, and an employee of a foreign embassy most definitely fell into that category. But this did not stop Albina. She did not fear the state and the threats of the security service, the so-called Sigurimi, *who were hastily hunting down 'enemies of the state' in Tirana, because they knew that the times were changing. Albina and George, a Greek Romeo and an Albanian Juliette, responded to each other's love, making themselves vulnerable and risking their lives. Due to the rapid opening of the country they were not sacrificed, but could build a life together, a family. During the past decades, thanks to George's work, Albina, as the wife of a diplomat, has travelled and lived in many countries around the world. Years ago she used to write to me that she would 'freeze' her feelings of missing home until she would have the opportunity to get back to Albania or until we would manage to meet again somewhere else. Nowadays Albina lives in Tirana, together with her husband and her son Arber. Our friendship has survived the years. I know for sure that my friend, inasmuch as she knows how to drift with the flow, keeps strong like a rock wherever she goes.*

I'm a daughter, a mother, a companion. For me being 'the daughter of' is equal to being a princess; being 'the wife of' is equal to being a woman; and being 'the mother of' equals eternity. Let me explain the daughter–princess relationship. My home was my castle. My mother and father were 'the guardians' who would defend the castle from any possible invasion and would not allow their princess to get hurt. All potential 'witches' with poisoned apples would turn into dust because of my parents. I had only to imagine a world of mine where things were going as I wished. Mentally I was free to do so, so why not? Being still a daughter, I became a mother and I understood that I've been lucky. Lucky, because you can't choose your parents. It is a lottery.

Being 'the wife of' is for me equal to being a woman. I was always afraid of marriage. I felt it was a great responsibility, charged with heavy routine that one can't escape. Day after day my individuality and that of my husband would fade away like rags exposed and forgotten in the sun. We would fade away to the point that one could not distinguish who was who any longer. But in becoming the life companion and the wife of George, I've discovered myself in all my female completeness. It is not that I was not aware of my femininity earlier, but now I'm a constant witness to being a woman, I have a constant 'teaser', a furnace where I melt, and a cooling system where I shrink, an ebb and a flow, energy and matter. And then I always have this image of us, walking down the street in the evening, our shadows on the pavement, sometimes touching each other, sometimes overlapping, sometimes keeping far apart, and still two shadows.

For me, being a mother means eternity. So there is eternity, precisely because there is procreation and there are children. When I will no longer be on this planet, I will still continue to live through my son. This is the strangest, the most beautiful and the most unexpected aspect of motherhood that I've experienced. On the one hand, motherhood made me realise that I'm not the 'owner' and master of my life, so I can't do with my life whatever I want. I can't lose myself, I can't 'bring an end' to myself, and 'lose' my life for caprice. My life is also my son's life. I had never thought so and still wonder why and how this happens. Whenever life has put me in difficulties, my child has been my liberation. I thought that when you are in difficult situations, having a child would make the situation that much harder, but the opposite has happened. Everything seems easier to achieve. One may ask why does this happen? I don't have the answer to that, except to refer to the cliché: 'A child is a gift of God'.

The first thing that comes to my mind when I think what makes me different is that I have blonde hair. I was the only cabbage head at school and in the neighbourhood. If it was only for this nickname, it would not matter. But this particularity had consequences. During my childhood all the games we played were with 'Partisans and Germans'. Due to my blonde hair, I was always assigned to play 'the cruel German'. 'I was German yesterday, can I please be a partisan today?' I would ask. My request fell on deaf ears and I would get the same response again and again: 'There are no blond partisans. If you want to play: be a German'. So in my subconsciousness there was a sense of guilt, being blonde meant for me being German, that's to say: hateful and bad. I became so obsessed with this, that in my second grade of elementary school, my childhood friend Shpëtime and I decided to colour our hair pitch black, painting it with shoe polish, which used to be sold in those round plastic boxes. Fortunately, Shpëtime's mum got home early that day and put the big boiler on the fire (the one she used to wash the sheets in), warmed the water and gave us a bath in their garden. And so I remained a guilty blonde.

Another particularity of those days was the 'private' house we lived in. It had a big garden, and a field of thousands of metres, surrounded by poplars and full of wild grass, weeds and wild flowers in purple, yellow and white. It was not only special. For me that was freedom: freedom to be one with nature. In the natural space I felt free. Moreover, there were no cars then to interrupt our play, there were no construction works to limit our territory and pollute our breath, there were no 'unknown' strangers to scare us. We were free to feel like the children of nature.

A liberating particularity was having my own room, which I didn't have to share with anyone. There I could read my books that I borrowed from the library. Some had to be read in secrecy. I wish everyone had a room of his/her own, from the day of birth until the last day of his/her life. In my opinion, having your personal room, an undivided space, gives to the individual the utmost freedom. In your personal space you do not have to follow the rules set by others for you. You can be yourself. '20:30, in bed and asleep, lights off'. I didn't like to have my light turned off, because I wanted to see the moth dancing around the light or wanted to play with the shadow of my hands and make animal figures. And even if the light was switched off, I didn't have to go to sleep. A room which is all yours allows you to develop your individuality. Being an individual for me is freedom. Becoming an individual in your childhood means having no fear to show your individuality when you grow up.

It's understandable that in certain times and situations, I was obliged to hide, to control, to camouflage my individuality. Often I had to appear to be different from what I was, I had to appear to be what I should be, but in fact what I wasn't. This is because I had to live – most of the time, if not all the time – in a group, in a 'collective'. It was impossible to lead your life and have time for yourself, because you were observed all the time. For me, leaving home in order to follow the secondary school in Tirana at the age of 14 was rather dramatic, precisely for this reason. I experienced it as a loss of freedom, sharing a room with six people in a dormitory. Long, never-ending corridors, with rooms on each side, all with unicolor blankets and white sheets and a radio that never stopped delivering state talks. The six of us shared a white bucket, and one water-heater coil, which looked like a torture tool used by the Gestapo in the books I read. The guardians entered and visited the rooms unannounced at all times of day and night, and the dull canteen fed us with the same food every day. I experienced moments of panic at the thought that after a while, we would all start looking the same.

Who were these unknown girls in whose company I slept every night? Who was I to them? How much of myself should I reveal? Should I be careful and not talk in my sleep? I could not tolerate life in the dorm and so I soon left to live with my aunt, where I found myself in a room of my own. Occasionally, thereafter, I would go at my own free will to the dorm, and spend time there with my friends. I had a good time then, because I was not obliged to stay and to be part of it.

Now that I tell you this, it feels as if I was an antisocial being. I love people, I love them a lot, but people organised in a 'collective' terrify me. The group, the collective in general, had something cruel, because it had more the tendency to attack and to bring about the war hysteria, rather than peace and wisdom.

People lose their freedom especially out of fear. We fear that we might eventually end up homeless, with no food, no job, no friends, no love. But our biggest fear is the fear of death. Because even if we would not think about it, death is hidden deep in our subconsciousness, it poisons and enslaves us all. It makes us conscious and rational. Every time you think of trying to jump with a parachute from an airplane, the fear of death whispers 'no'; every time you would like to whack some people on the head, the fear of 'the electric chair' symbolically says 'no'; each time you would like to blow up some ugly buildings, architectonically and symbolically, again you hear 'no'; also because you never know if you would blow yourself up too. How many times did you want to dive into the ocean and swim alongside the sharks, and the fear of death said 'no'...

These are extreme examples, but I've met with death a few times. The first time I was a child, at sea. I could swim very well. At some point after swimming far away from the coast, I decided to return. When I got nearer, I thought I could touch the ground with the tips of my toes, and could rest. I was sure it was not deep, but I had miscalculated. It was deep and the water covered me completely. I panicked, forgot how to swim and drank a lot of seawater. And the more I tried recalling how to swim, the more I forgot how to do so. I drank and drank. After some moments I stopped struggling and got quiet, opened my eyes and as I was drowning I looked around me. The water had a violet colour and was full of big golden sea stars. Those saved me. They gave me the strength to pull myself together, go up and swim towards the coast.

Later, it was the Secret Service who gave me the undeserved opportunity to fear death. But I escaped once more and I was again free to be 'stupid', free to laugh, to express myself, to enjoy life, to appreciate a leaf falling on my shoulder, liberated from envy, unhealthy ambitions, and jealousy. I was free to love myself the way I am, free to love people the way they are. To lose the fear of death means gaining the freedom of an angel.

There are plenty of events that have influenced me and have made me grow up. First, I was around seven or eight years old and we used to live very near the sea. It was a hot night in August when we decided to take a swim, around midnight. I dove into the sea and with my eyes open could notice many twinkling jellyfish round me. I stayed for about an hour in the water: going up, breathing and then again diving and following the jellyfish. I was far away from the people and the coast. When I got back, I didn't listen to all the angry remarks and the shouting. I had only one thought: 'God had decided to show me and only me this wonderful secret'. I was convinced that miracles happen.

Second, I was twelve years of age and had a little brown dog named Tommy. I felt connected with him, also because I never had such a small and daring dog. Some men from the Vlora municipality, all armed with guns and rifles, killed him with five bullets. It was part of an 'action' and an order given from above to clean the streets of the city. From that time on I fear only people, not the darkness, not beasts.

And the third one was when I was 22 years old. I was arrested by the Secret Service, because of my love 'affair' with George, who worked at the Greek Embassy. They pushed me inside their truck and I found myself among six ugly men. As I thought about how this would end – most probably being dragged by a car at Tirana's main boulevard until I would die – in spite of considering all their threats, I somehow felt an utter peace inside myself. All the anxiety, the terror and the panic disappeared. I had learned how to subdue fear.

The first and the third encounters have given me a sense of freedom, whereas the killing of my little dog constrained and limited me. I often isolate and detach myself deliberately. I also often feel like talking with all the fools of the town, who wander in the streets. Maybe I find my balance somewhere in between those two acts.

❋

Do I feel Albanian? At times, that question seems absurd to me. Perhaps travelling, as well as living in different parts of the world has made me realise that I'm part of a whole universe, as much as the universe is within me.

Am I Albanian because I have dreams and desires, because I cry and get desperate, because I grieve and shout, because I can relax and enjoy life as an Albanian? No. I don't think so. I think that mankind as a whole functions emotionally more or less in the same way. Tears and smiles do not have a nationality, that is why I just feel like any other human being on earth. The feeling of being Albanian is and was conditioned by the state, as a way of organising the life of the Albanians. Through the existence of the state, I know and knew that I'm Albanian. Again due to this definition I can judge whether this state does better or worse than others. I felt that I was an Albanian citizen, when I first used the escalator. I was 24 years old and had to learn this simple trick. The Albanian state did not approve of its citizens using the escalator. It is the same sensation and feeling I had when as an Albanian citizen – unlike a Greek citizen, an Italian or an American – I was prevented from crossing borders and visiting other countries.

Maybe I'm not able to clearly define the difference between nationality and citizenship. The one you are born with and the other you attain later. Today what matters and what defines you more is the second.

❋

I didn't get the Greek citizenship out of need. Thanks to the fact that I was a wife of a diplomat, I didn't have to queue for a visa. How do I see this issue? The willingness and persistence of many compatriots to obtain another citizenship has been a matter of concern for me. I often asked myself if it was worth the struggle and all the compromises? Why was there such haste necessary in changing the last name, if possible also the first name? Unfortunately, it's all justifiable. Having a new citizenship was considered a condition for all those who left the homeland, so that they could move freely, could settle with a job, could have a better life. What is painful is what we do not often talk about – though we all know it – and that is the necessary denial of being the way you are, of the self. Getting another citizenship was equal, if not an effort, to detach, and to remove from yourself the stigma of being 'Albanian', which is unfortunately seen by some as a 'curse'. By obtaining another citizenship it seemed as if you could wash off yourself this country's history, the years you lived here, unjustly, in isolation and in misery. It was an effort to get rid of the poverty, the crime, the prostitution, the drugs with which being 'Albanian' has often been associated in the last decades. So another citizenship meant, and is something more than just having, freedom of movement in the world. It was wiping off all the maladies of our past, and cleansing ourselves from being considered as carriers of those maladies.

I dragged my feet getting the Greek citizenship. Nothing special, but precisely because I felt I was denying myself the 'right' to live all over the world as an Albanian. And this had nothing to do with patriotism, but with something else. Certainly I was privileged, being the wife of a diplomat, compared to the hundreds of Albanian migrants, sisters and brothers, known and unknown. My reasoning or the emotion affecting me taking a decision had to do with something personal. At the end of the day, being from Albania, my country, where I used to live, felt special. I felt like a rare species. There are only 3 million Albanians, while the world population is around 7.3 billion people. Is it not something strange to give up such a rare citizenship?

I got the Greek citizenship with the same name and surname that I use in my Albanian passport. I didn't find it necessary to change my name. Maybe because I never felt I was Greek, even though my husband is Greek. This doesn't mean that I don't love the Greeks or that I'm anti-Greek. Every nation has its own greatness and its own obscurities and mediocrities.

The connecting threads and ties with Albania, my country, are my parents, the land, the property, the nature and my friends. The two special things that I consider important are: the Albanian tables – when you get together around the table you can be whoever you like in Albania. Everything becomes possible around the table. You become a millionaire, a Prime Minister, a famous rock singer, the Pope, the victim, the executed and the hangman. I love the Albanian tables passionately. Second, I like that in Albania's cities, it takes one only 3 minutes to go from point A to B; and only 30 minutes to get from point A to Z – I like the fact that you do not lose time on the way just to reach your destination.

Albania doesn't tolerate one being oneself, not to mention that Albania often condemns or exploits you for being yourself. And to add to that, it ridicules and mocks you loudly or silently for being yourself.

Albania has obliged me to become a responsible grown-up, but this tendency distances me from Albania rather than bringing me nearer to her. To grow up, in the Albanian sense of the word, unfortunately is to be a bit of all these: 'blackleg', 'a spy', 'revengeful', 'snitch', 'rogue', 'clown'. In other words: to outsmart the other and be in conflict with the other. I don't want to develop in this way. But Albania imposes this kind of growth upon all its citizens.

I never felt a lady or master of my country. Never! I feel a lady and master of my own house. But I can feel at home in every country of the world. Here in Albania, I've always felt like a guest, a guest expected to take the assigned seat, to greet the masters of the house and to shake their hands. To greet those masters, whom I might not respect. One has no choice but to greet them from the chair where I've been seated, a chair that has my name on it, me part of a crowd I don't want to be with. Albania's feasts are always given by few masters of the country, greedy masters who leave no room for me to feel that I'm also a master of this house which is actually ours. You might ask: Why did I return to Albania then? Among other reasons, because I still hope to one day feel like a lady of my own country.

I actually live where I want to live, in Albania. The country is an endless stress, but the stress is the salt and pepper of life. Albania remains a special experience even for us, the Albanians. Perhaps it resembles a laboratory where endless experiments are carried out, although you know that almost all of them will fail, still for one reason or another you want to be part of that experiment. What if the experiment has the chance to succeed as well? How could you afford not having been part of this miracle?

For me being part of a community is equal to the collective, equal to being brainwashed, it's the end of individual authenticity. Well, it's still interesting to note that we can do without the community. I didn't feel the need to be part of the Albanian community abroad. I also did not live abroad with the desire to repeat or to find Albania elsewhere.

It looks to me that mankind is bound and connected by certain truths, if we can call them universal, considering that we all cry and laugh at the same things, being South Africans, Americans or Albanians like myself. We experience joy, happiness and despair in the same way, we are moved by the same things, and we always wish for something better than what we have. We fear the same things, we all dance to the sound of music, and it doesn't really matter if we live in a skyscraper in New York or in a stand-alone house in the steppe or here in the New Tirana district.

Encountering different cultures and different ways of life in the countries where you have lived was really miraculous. I felt like an actress that had to change the director, the producer and the rest of the crew, while performing on new stages. Life was so diverse that there was no time to get bored.

I don't know if this really counts, but I think the world is very small. It should have been at least 12 times bigger, with 13 moons, each one a different colour.

I often think I will never die. If I will die, I will die because of my passions. Because I'm passionate even about the simplest thing that I do, any kind of job or even walking down the street. I get completely involved, I observe the pavement, where it rises and I think about the roots of the tree under it, I imagine a colony of ants, the danger of falling. In the clouds I always see lots of figures and events happening. When I swim I observe and enjoy the appearance and disappearance of the lines in the sand, when I skate I think human beings could fly but we have not yet figured out how. When I play basketball I feel I have so much energy as to thrust the ball to the sky where it would stay and become a moon. In short, every moment I live with passion.

I do believe in God. At different moments I call God, the Universe, the Energy. I believe in God because I believe in the creation, in this balanced and perfect creation. I believe in God and in the creation of the world! I believe in God also because I believe in 'no beginning' and 'no end', I believe in God because I'm me, you are you and we are both here at this moment. I see how wonderful and how incomprehensible the work of God is. It is the mystery of life itself. I exist because God exists!

I've never worked fixed hours, for example from 9 am to 4 pm. If I had to, I would have hated it. I don't like discipline. I'm lucky that all I do – giving advice as a makeup consultant and stylist, dealing with the courts regarding property issues – I do these things at my own pace and I decide about the timing. Another issue is that all that we do turns into routine. This makes works unbearable. Personally, I would have liked to learn new skills and professions every two to three years. I like to work, but I like to do various things, that allow me to express myself, my imagination and creativity.

※

I'm proud that I never had idols, not even in my childhood. Ordinary people with a simple life, with a big heart, incredible wisdom, who are able to give so much love and with endless passions each time I meet them – they become important to me. I would not exaggerate if I would say that I learned much more from them, rather than from all my school books, about kindness, wisdom, and innocent madness.

※

Reflecting on the past, on the old system and way of life, I see it as a period of many lost years. I feel contempt for that inhuman system. When I recall those times I really hate it all! In the first place that it did not allow my grandmother, my mother, my aunts, my teachers, my girlfriends to feel like women! I can't forget or ignore the fact that we came from a feudal and backward society. The communist dictatorship, different from its propaganda and the speeches of the leaders, caused a real drama. For me, its drive to harshen, to roughen and 'de-womanise' the women was an unforgivable crime, because you can't rule a society efficiently where half the population is totally dehumanised and de-womanised. We used to live in a system that controlled everything, even the hormones of youth. Perhaps they are all lost years, but they are my years, which I carry with me forever. That is why I don't know if I can consider them as lost, something that I always carry with me.

Many things must change in Albania. First of all, they have to forbid spying, any kind of spying that is to the detriment of the individual and does not really benefit society. Let us not 'target' or 'nail to the cross' the individual, let us not destroy his or her life for personal gains. The rest of us are not angels. Second, let us not be afraid to be ourselves, and at the same time let us accept the courage of the other to be oneself. Let us not use the qualities they have to fight them. And finally, let us forbid once and for all the applauding of the people at the end of the politicians' speeches, independent of the party they represent! Let us applaud only works of art and heroic human deeds.

How would I like Albania to be in 30 years? It's utopia, but I'll give it a try. First of all, I would like to see an Albania without untidy and muddled wires. Have you noticed all the electric poles full of wires above our heads? Our vision of the sky would be clearer without them. Then I want to see the roofs of the houses, with no water reservoirs. I want to have at least seven good roads, with no holes, in every city. Each one would be at least 1 kilometre. I would like to see city squares full of colourful parrots. I would like to see town gardens and parks, full of wild flowers that grow in our region.

Not in this order of priority, I certainly want a European Albania (actually, it should have become a member of the European Union a long time ago) whose people abide by the law and whose politicians have matured. No doubt I want an Albania where the economy is developed and the standard of life is high. In fact, I think we should already have most of these things right now.

And I've not mentioned that justice should have long been done about things that belong to us, such as the question of property rights.

Something else: I wish a discovery would be made so that some writing in the Illyrian language is documented. We would feel good, when we would be able to verify our continuity and antiquity, which in fact is recognised and proven in other ways.

Finally, I wish we would keep our own Balkan temperament when at the table. So keep being loud and blissfully gay.

Andrea

> *The future depends on what we do in the present.*
> Mahatma Gandhi

It is October. Outside the wind blows and the leaves fall. My train stops at every station of the past. Now it will stop at Andrea Bënja's.

This train of mine collects many dear people at Andrea's station: Andrea, his wife Luiza, their daughters Anisa and Jola, Andrea's sister, Mrs Irini, who taught me algebra, Luiza's sister Mimoza, whose voice and humour are so recognisable. Two other dear people are also central to this encounter – Auntie Liliana and Uncle Sybi. Uncle Sybi passed away some years ago but, as is often the case with people who are together for a long time, at the first sight of Liliana, I see Uncle Sybi too. I recall him, bald and smiling, telling stories about his hometown, Gjirokastra.

Andrea is in charge at this station. With his knowledge and his skills, he takes care to maintain it, regularly welcoming both old and new trains, each and every one loaded with memories.

Perhaps you might like to know where his station is? For many years now Andrea has built his nest in the heart of a forest, in a suburb of Toronto, in a region covered by snow for many months of the year. In my imagination, Uncas, the last of the Mohicans and a childhood hero, ran in those forests. Andrea has become a Canadian citizen. He has planted some Dutch tulips in his garden, and on this Sunday afternoon he is expecting some friends to pay him a visit. He and Luiza have many old and new friends. Some old friends Andrea worked alongside in the huge tractor factory 'Enver Hoxha' in Tirana. They have all moved to Canada. When evening falls, Andrea will make a fire. He will probably take out his guitar and play some well-known melodies from his homeland.

Andrea is an engineer. I got to know him as a teenager. In those days I was more familiar with journalists and teachers, so as an *engineer he had some mystery attached to him. Science, physics, chemistry and algebra were all tangible and intelligible to Andrea. There was also something mysterious and attractive about the fact that he had studied for years in the Far East, in China. Albanians of my generation, living as we did in a large village surrounded by barbed wire, dreamed about visiting America, London, Paris, Rome and Vienna. Our parents were nostalgic about Moscow and Sofia. Andrea had gone instead to the unknown vastness that was China, first to Beijing and then later to Shenyang. His bookshelves housed many stout paperbacks whose titles were written in beautiful 'secret' Chinese characters. It seemed to me that when Andrea spoke quietly in his pure literary Albanian, somewhere deep inside his voice I heard the gurgling of the Chinese language and the wisdom of Confucius.*

All this made Andrea uniquely attractive and mysterious. Feel free to add a hefty dose of admiration that a sixteen-year-old girl might feel for her guitar teacher.

In those days, pre-1990, many things were done by 'volunteers' – ditch digging, olive and corn harvesting, cleaning public spaces, even giving extra lessons to 'backward' pupils. It was all drudgery, a millstone around the neck of anyone called upon to fulfill these tasks by the Party, the State, the Democratic Front or the School. Andrea, on the other hand, actually volunteered, out of his own free will, to teach me guitar once a week. Every Sunday morning, he carried his bike up five floors to our apartment just to listen to me play.

Andrea was known to be a good, hard-working family man, well-organised and, above all, passionate. His passions were what we call hobbies today. He always found time not only to work hard and to support his wife Luiza, but to play football with his friends and play guitar. To me, a dreamy, lazy and unsystematic teenager, Andrea was a model man. I started learning to play guitar but stopped short when I fell head over heels in love with a boy who spoke and recited beautifully. All I can remember of my guitar les-

sons are two classical pieces and some chords with which I can still accompany the Shkodra's song White Hortensia or the Beatles' song Ob-La-Di, Ob-La-Da.

A few years ago Luiza and Andrea paid me a visit in Amsterdam when they were travelling through Europe. I remember Andrea doing three things. He examined a map of The Netherlands with the dedication of a man who wanted to discover the secret code of the Dutch capacity to subdue water. Then, with the same interest and enthusiasm, he read from beginning to end my collection of poetry which had just been published in Tirana, and finally, after seeing the city, Andrea and Luiza even attended a gathering of my fellow journalists to talk about the short-lived war in Georgia and the role of the media in the conflict. This was in August 2008 after a hopeless and unequal war resulted in the secession of South Ossetia from Georgia. Andrea made a real effort to follow the debate and understand the reasons behind the first European war of the 21st century. He remains curious, serious and committed, and has an extraordinary eye for detail. For this reason, it is impossible for me not to stop at his 'station' today to have this talk.

My father was the son of a medical doctor, though he did not have much education himself. My grandfather was known to be an important man who played a role in the negotiations about the borders of Albania. Pano, our neighbour in Tirana, used to say to me: 'Hi Bënja, good morning. Did you have a good night's rest?' And then, rather unexpectedly, he would add: 'Your grandfather was a great man. The newspapers wrote about him when he went to negotiate in Greece.' Little was left of his engagement or his glory after the liberation of Albania in 1944, and my father, whose business was trade, lost all his money at that time. His house was damaged in the bombing of Përmet during the Greco-Italian war, so he came to Tirana with a bunch of children.

All of us went to university. Upon graduation, two of my

sisters were appointed to work in Kruja. I remember them crying, not wanting to go there because it was a hell of a road and there were transport difficulties at that time. I took a somewhat different path. Instead of finishing school I started working when I was 15 years old. Prof. Krasta from Elbasan, a good musician who taught me guitar, advised me to attend the Artistic Lyceum. 'No way!' I said, with my sisters' desperation in mind. I didn't want to become a teacher and have to work in a village, so I decided instead to work at the electromechanical plant, and attend evening classes for the next four years. My maths teacher, seeing my results, asked me to consider attending day school. 'No, no, I need to work because of the economic situation', I answered. There was no real economic need but I was afraid I would end up working in a village.

I worked for four years at the plant, not really knowing why I chose to do so. When I watched students walking down the street in a leisurely way, while I was dressed as a worker, I realised it was my own doing. At night school I got good marks, with an average of 9.8, so finally I applied to study mechanical engineering at the university, and I won a place. My name was seventh on the list. It was a stressful period, but one which brought results. At the end of the terms, I organised seminars. I was young and somewhat withdrawn and I had no clue how the system worked. For me, it remains a puzzle how I was accepted to university – coming from night school – and how I was later selected to go to China. Although I should say that the group of students who went to China was a mixed bunch. Some had parents in good 'positions' in the party and were of good social standing, some were 'ordinary' like me.

I like to call a spade a spade. This may seem a bit contradictory in view of the fact that I'm quite withdrawn – but it's my nature, and, as such, I don't have a lot of friends, but the few friendships I have are long lasting.

Before I went to China, we kept in touch with my father's relatives in France by correspondence. My mother's relatives were in America, but with them we could not really correspond. Albania was still closed. Our only window on the world was Italy. People dreamt of going to Italy, but when they finally went they were disappointed. The world they saw on their TV screens was different from the one they had to deal with as immigrants.

The time I spent studying in China was perhaps the most beautiful period of my life. China was 'another world', especially for us Albanian students who left the country during one of the darkest periods of its communist history. In those days Albania was becoming even more isolated. It was the end of a short liberal spring, with Paçrami, Lubonja and Luarasi, and with the 11th Song Festival in the Albanian Public Radio and Television[1]. Artists and intellectuals dreamed that Albania would open up to the world. Instead, only more isolation came. A break with China was anticipated. China was opening up to the West, which was seen as a betrayal of Marxism-Leninism.

I remember our first evening in Beijing, with hundreds of students from all over the world performing, sharing the art and music of their countries. It was something completely new and different, seeing and listening to unknown musical instruments and languages. After that evening, we Albanian students were often joined by a bearded young Scandinavian and a beautiful girl from Yugoslavia. It was really a laboratory where different people, cultures, thoughts and ways of life could intermingle. You would see a group of North Koreans, with their loud voices and emblems of Kim Il Sung on their chests, constantly studying; you would see a group of students selected by the Japanese government communicating, with some difficulty, with another group of Japanese brought by the China-Japan Friendship Association; an Austrian student who had with him the sheet music of Bob Dylan's songs; Western students in blue jeans who were always reading wherever they went; a French student who started to learn Albanian and tried to practice it on us nonstop; a German student who took pride in the fact that his father was a pilot during World War II and asked intelligent questions about anti-aircraft guns in the factory we visited. In short, in the big world of China there was room for everybody.

We really felt it to be a huge and ancient country when we visited the Thirteen Tombs of the Ming Dynasty near Beijing, or when we walked along the Great Wall and read the names of Albanians who had been there before us, when we listened for the first time to the Beijing Symphony Orchestra with their five-tone musical scale, when we saw images of the Buddha, or when a Chinese student talked to us with acupuncture needles stuck in his temples to relieve a headache. What impressed me as well was how the Chinese managed to interweave their ancient culture with modern culture in everyday life.

We got to know the country during our vacations, on tourist trips and internships. We would leave our city dressed in heavy coats to travel south to a place where the climate was hot. Many foreign students posted to the south preferred not to go back home even during the holiday season.

Of course we were dreamers. It was strange and incomprehensible to us to observe that the same city which punished Deng Xiaoping later supported him, to listen to the non-stop funeral music which was broadcast for Mao Zedong, to see how the so-called Gang of Four were destroyed. China was huge and complicated. The Chinese are now putting into practice the visions of Zhou Enlai and Deng Xiaoping. During our stay we saw how the old catalogues and engineering manuals that we used were replaced in no time with news of the latest scientific developments. At the same time Albania was becoming more isolated, more autocratic and closed, it was 'dancing in the wolf's mouth' as the expression goes. When the Chinese installed machinery of the highest technical specification in Albanian plants, the Albanians complained of sabotage.

We were serious in our studies. Often our teachers and the Chinese specialists they brought in were surprised by our questions, thinking we had already had a specialisation of some sort in Albania. We learned a lot about science in China. We lived as if in a dream but we matured. We experienced life in different communities, both big and small, we experienced difficult situations, but we also experienced a great joy and we got to know a very different world and culture. That is why I'm convinced that studying in China made me the person I'm today. I lived there for four and half years, from 1973 to 1978, when relations between the two countries finally broke down.

When I returned to Albania I tried to get used to living here again. There was nothing else to do but to accept the situation as it was. Albania continued to go from bad to worse, entering an even darker period with the punishments that followed the death of the premier Mehmet Shehu. The best times are often considered best because they are followed by the worst. I was depressed after China. I thought my life was over. I was assigned to work in the auto-tractor factory. I didn't know anyone there, nor did I know the process because I was not trained to work in that sector. I was working in Tirana and was sent to a village where I expected to work with a group of specialists who studied bauxite. I went to Korça and met some scientists working there, but the process was in an experimental phase and so I could not do much there. I was then appointed to work with steel, and not with alloys or aluminium about which I knew a lot more because of my research.

After six months, just as I was beginning to fit in there, I was sent to Burrel, where the ferro-chromium factory was starting production. I travelled up and down there for a while, and I eventually explained to the cadres office that it was pointless because I didn't know much about ferro-chromium. Their answer was that the need determined where I would work. They needed construction engineers as well as mechanical engineers and it was up to the party to make the decisions! Indeed, everyone who graduated or had a specialisation in those days could find a job, but not always in the field in which they had graduated or were interested.

After a meaningless period of drifting I returned to the auto-tractor factory and settled down there. It was out of the question for me to continue with postgraduate studies abroad. As an individual my career was in the hands of the cohort in charge of cadre politics. All I could do was follow a postgraduate program at the University of Tirana and teach at the Faculty of Engineering, so I did that. During those years at the factory, I did achieve something. I studied and I experimented with aluminium connections, making main parts of the automobile, such as the piston. I defended my thesis with this study, which is recognised here in Canada.

I remember once we sent an order to Hungary and there

were problems with the parts that arrived. A specialist had to be sent to evaluate what could be done. I went to Hungary, resolved the issue and asked to see the process of piston production in the factory. Though Hungary was part of the Socialist Bloc, it was the showcase of the East, proud of its traditions, with beautiful monuments and luxurious palaces. We Albanians were hungry for colour, impressed even by the colourful bottles that soft drinks came in. When travelling abroad, we felt sad amid the abundance and the spectacle, because you can't take that beauty back home with you. I don't mean just the form or the veneer but the way of life, the fibre of society. So it wasn't only in the West, but also in the East, that people lived differently from us. We were nowhere. We were behind the world.

The beginning of the nineties was a difficult period. Work at the auto-tractor factory was suspended. The government had no idea how to plan for the future, what to do with the factory, which had been a gigantic investment for a small country like Albania. The business could not be rescued because the so-called businessmen of that time, our pseudo merchants, could not manage such a big enterprise. The factory became derelict, systematically damaged and plundered, and it seems this is still its status today.

I went to work at the Ministry of Health, as an engineer in charge of health equipment. It was not a bad job and not as exhausting as the factory. I recall that in 1997, when we distributed health equipment under fire and after the curfew, Luiza and I began to understand that we could successfully pursue our professions in either the United States or Canada. I got the chance to talk to colleagues in America when I was invited by my mother's family to a wedding in Massachusetts in 1995. I was offered work in my field while I was there, but we were not yet prepared, mentally or spiritually, to emigrate as a family. I returned to Tirana.

❖

I believe in God. I'm not an atheist. I think faith will continue to exist alongside science, as long as there is so much that is unknown. Mankind needs faith. I don't have faith in one thing alone. Faith is inside me, inside you, faith is the ideas we have about God. Faith is important. Many things are possible for people who have faith, just as long as faith and religion are not used purely instrumentally to obtain wealth and benefits. Religious institutions have their own value too. My mother kept her faith in God even when believers were persecuted in Albania.

When the country started to open up and change at the beginning of the nineties, many missionaries of various religious affiliations came to Albania. I was asked to translate the Bible – the parts of it that deal with forgiveness, reconciliation and healing. How can we forgive? This was very important for a society that was breaking down, ridding itself of a dictatorship, when many people wanted to settle old and new grievances by any means. The aggrieved party has to learn to forgive so that he or she can move forward. I translated some religious texts and for a while I was busy with some evangelists who wanted to inspire faith in a people who had been denied the right to believe. I think I didn't do badly. The evangelists were progressive in their religion because they had done away with the idea of a church hierarchy and talked instead about a direct connection with God.

In the beginning of the nineties, Albanians were seeking direction. There was a particular moment when I truly believed that if I really focused I would feel the mystery of the universe and I might achieve real spiritual peace. I think this was the most effective way of communicating with others after leaving darkness behind. It was 1991 or 1992 and I, like many others in Albania, was reconstructing my identity. I developed close relationships with English, German and especially some very dedicated Dutch evangelists. Together we visited remote villages, unreachable by road, so often we went by helicopter and distributed aid anonymously. I recall people living in extreme poverty behind Dajti mountain. It happened that criminal bands, often connected with local governors, persecuted the missionaries. Sadly so.

After I returned from the United States, Luiza and I decided to apply for permission to immigrate to Canada. 1997 found us still in Albania. At that time I would accompany foreign journalists who were travelling throughout the country reporting on the crisis, the madness that Albanians were caught up in after the fall of the pyramids[2]. In Vlora there were armed clashes, Fier was packed with barricades. When we tried to reach the South via Ballsh, the rebels, many of them young, blocked the road. Only foreigners were allowed to enter the region from the North.

The following day I was with a group of journalists who went to see what was happening near the offices of the Vefa company in Tirana. It was the events of March 1997 that put an end to my dilemma about whether to stay or leave. I wanted nothing more than to leave the madness behind as soon as possible. Canada approved our application without an interview. Demoralised by the perverse events of that year, we prepared to leave. We finally left Albania at the beginning of 1998, almost two decades ago.

We have become Canadians. At least, our daughters are Canadians while Luiza and I, because of how old we were when we immigrated, we are more Albanian than Canadian. We have become Canadian citizens, but we are still in transition. We are a generation in transition. Our daughters are more integrated. They say the second generation of immigrants still face difficulties but we, the parents, had to pay the price of moving, of change, of confrontation with a hundred unknowns. Being ignorant makes one afraid. There is no certainty how things will turn out, but we bear responsibility for our lives, we are no longer beholden to state and party.

I feel very much a European. I'm proud of it. In China I understood that our way of living in Europe, independent of our poverty in Albania, could not be compared with the way the Chinese live. As Europeans we waste carelessly and to no purpose. Although Albanians do not have a good name in the world today, I'm convinced that there is little difference between us and Italians, Polish, Croats or Slovenes. At the end of the day, it's the individual that matters in Europe and in the West. Things changed in Albania because individuals wanted to be free. I like the traditions of my country – they are different from other countries, even European ones – but if you talk about being identified as an Albanian, or as a European or as a world citizen, what matters in all cases is intellect and one's level of education.

Albania is little known here in Canada, except to other immigrants from the Eastern Bloc. When I talk with Slovenes and Croats I understand that they also lived to a certain degree in a closed system and that their way of thinking is similar to our Albanian way. This is the Balkan mentality.

The Italians, Chinese, Ukrainians and Poles first made it across to Canada a hundred years ago. Very few Albanians did so. That massive immigration a century ago meant that newly arriving Ukrainians and Italians had each other to rely on and they developed a powerful sense of community. We Albanians, few in number here today, do not have the benefit of community. However, if you are capable you can make it here as an individual.

It is important to understand how the system works. Upon arrival, we lacked even basic knowledge about the system. An Indian immigrant, who has been living in post-colonial India, knows how Anglo-Saxon capitalist societies function, what is expected from him, the framework for coexistence. He or she arrives with a clear idea about where he or she is heading, what is necessary to achieve success. We had no such point of reference. We were on our own, with no support whatsoever. We had to start from scratch.

I don't think it was a mistake to leave Albania. It might have been good to stay; but I would have more questions; or I would have worried that I should have tried my luck elsewhere. The move has been positive from a financial perspective. We started at zero, and it will take time before our daughters will be fully integrated, but Canada is a country of opportunity.

No doubt the Albanian society was patriarchal, but I personally felt its conservatism more. I was the youngest in my family and my older sisters were strong and capable. Even today Luiza drives more than I do – although they say it's men who can't let go of the wheel. I have never felt bad surrounded by strong women. My mother was from Përmet, a strong woman who knew how to run a household. My father was very soft, he would never give orders, he trusted us instead. He was proud of us. He did not see me as a problem and he never shouted. My parents and my sisters were very important in my life. I learned from my mother to be organised and disciplined. I have tried to transmit these values to my children. The decisive people in my life today are my wife Luiza and our daughters. Luiza is an optimist by nature, she is positive and forward-looking, always ready to face the challenges that we encounter. The girls are now grown up, they have finished their studies and are building their own nests here. Anisa has graduated from McGill University in Montreal, Jola graduated with a business degree from Toronto University. They have different characters and belong to a different generation, but they have always encouraged and supported our decisions.

If I were able to start again from scratch as a parent, I would behave differently with my children. I would communicate differently and more intensively with them. My own upbringing, my parents, the culture and system in Albania, all affected the way I behaved as a parent. I should have been more engaged with my children. I should have encouraged them to be more independent and more responsible. I see parents here relate very differently to their children. But in the end what happens also depends on a child's character.

My typical day in Canada is a workers' day. I spend most of my time working. I start at 7 am and return home around 6 pm. Every day I travel 120 kilometres. For the past 12 years I've worked for the same company, 'Purity Zinc Metals'. It is a stable business and I enjoy working there. After dinner I go walking with Charlie, our dog and good friend. We talk to him more in English than in Albanian and have taught him to be sociable, although he is a Yorkie and remains somehow wild and defensive. He has such a combative spirit in his little body.

The most beautiful days start on Friday evening and go through the weekend. We get together with friends. This benign tradition has broken down a bit recently because we have lost Pirro, a very good old friend of ours. We are trying to find a new balance with his widow, but it's not the same without Pirro, with whom Luiza and I worked for many years in Albania.

The weekend starts quietly, with an espresso and sometimes also a fernet. I can't ignore my age and one glass of fernet gives me some energy and pulls me together. I prefer to rest on Saturday. In the evening we sometimes get together with friends again and all go drinking and dancing. Another pleasure is to spend time with our daughters and their friends, sometimes here in the house, sometimes outdoors.

When spring comes I'm busy gardening. We spend a lot of time outdoors. We often have lunch in the garden. Luiza is very fond of camping. We have gone camping at frezing temperature at the end of September. When the sun came out we swam and dove. We all go camping together, young and old. There are many places to camp here in provincial and national parks. It is just as the Ontario license plates have it: 'Yours to be discovered'. When we first arrived I used to think: What is there to find and explore here? But Canada is full of beautiful places. The problem is the summer is very short, we don't have long to enjoy the beautiful beaches and the lakes.

Today we started the day with a long walk in the forest. The urban areas are well wooded. You can clearly see the difference between those urban planners who are inclined to destroy and those who are inclined to build and preserve. If a tree has fallen, the municipal team try hard to revive it while making sure that people can move uninhibited around it. This is very different from where we come from, where even the handle on a water tap is stolen so that it may be sold. I think it has to do with citizenship. If a person drops something personal here, the chances are that someone will find it and put it aside in a visible place so that the owner can retrieve it.

Community feeling and citizenship together. It may be that this happens because people fear the police. In Canada and the United States police are fully empowered. You can't play with the police here. But I think that being a citizen is more than fear and an exercise of violence. It means taking an active part in society, respecting your community, taking responsibility.

It's not easy to adapt and to change your identity. People want to feel proud of where they come from, where they were mentally and spiritually shaped, but I think Canada and the United States are countries in which both integration and respect for the immigrant's national identity are possible. We have to pay the price of immigrating, but returning to Albania today might be a great disappointment. We feel okay here. Taxes are high but you can resolve bureaucratic problems easily, our children have a future and each one of us feels fulfilled in his or her own way. I do try to feel part of the whole here.

I vote, especially when it concerns important issues for our local community. Some time ago I took part in some meetings in which the building of new apartments was discussed. The residents were against the idea. I was neither a great enthusiast nor a fervent opponent, but I considered it important to be informed about what was happening around us. We also like to celebrate the national holidays. We celebrate them all. And I'm fond of Canadian basketball, hockey and football, as well as of Italian football.

I have dreams, but I don't really fight to pursue them. I would like to live in a warmer climate, at least during the winter months. For now, it's out of question because we are both working. I would really like to work as long as I can, at least until I'm 70. The kind of job I have now I will still be able to do at that age. Perhaps when we retire we'll consider moving south, or travelling to the Caribbean or to Florida in a recreational vehicle, which are widely used here. Perhaps we'll go to Albania. Because we need the sun.

I've thought of returning to Albania. It's possible. I miss Albania. It's many years now since we left, so I would like to try and live there again. Albania has changed for the better. It may happen that the issues related to property – in our case in Përmet – will be resolved. We would then buy an apartment by the sea in Himara. If we had our property returned to us, we would go with pleasure. It is a nice dream. But nothing is fixed or final, these are simply possibilities. If you do not have dreams, you are finished. And certainly my dreams are connected with Luiza and our daughters.

Some things would have to be in place for me to return. First, the rule of law, so that there is a functioning system, and the property issue resolved sooner rather than later. Until now all parties in power have shared one common denominator: they have thought only of how to enrich themselves at the expense of others; they have not resolved the issue of personal property. It may be due to the fact that they are products of the same kitchen, but a solution has to be found because it's the only way that Albania will find balance, harmony and opportunities for all Albanians. This is what I dream about and I'm not alone in this.

Gazi

> My dear fellow, who will let you?
> That's not the point. The point is, who will stop me?
> Ayn Rand: *The Fountainhead*

'Let me tell you what I'm doing now', says Gazi, as we take a seat in a quiet area at the Hotel Rogner in Tirana on a pleasant summer afternoon. He starts with a long list of projects that he is working on together with Anila, his wife who is also his partner in business. Together they lead a company of 85 people.

Everytime we meet, Gazi lists his achievements speedily, and I am impressed with everything he tells me, though sometimes I can hardly recall where he was yesterday and where he is heading to in the early hours of the next day. Gazi is continuously on the road. Last year he spent at least 140 days on the road, flying all over the globe. This time I am prepared and have taken a recorder with me – so that my memory will not let me down.

I listen to his voice, the numbers, the sums and the names of places he has visited, the names of prestigious universities he has lectured at, the names of business centres he has consulted. Gazi likes to talk about all of this. Now and then he shares a joke and this river of achievements becomes relative. This is how it used to be, this is how it still is.

Dear readers: most of the information that I have recorded can be found online, because Gazmend Haxhia is a known public figure in Albania and abroad. In 2008 he was selected as a 'Young Global Leader' by the World Economic Forum. Gazi has a master's degree in International Affairs from Columbia University and he further educated himself at INSEAD Fontainebleau and Harvard Business School. Gazi is the owner of Opel and Avis car rental companies in Albania, founder and investor of the guide Tirana in Your Pocket *and co-founder of POLIS University, where each year 100 students graduate. He also sits on the board of several institutions in Albania, Kosovo, and the Balkans.*

He is the father of two beautiful children and the husband of an ambitious and emancipated woman. Trying to keep in touch with the 'Flying Gazi' has often only been made possible through the intervention of Anila.

Why then do I want Gazi to have his own chapter in this book, which mainly focuses on memory and deals with remembering and still forgetting, where time is suspended and the rhythm of the past mingles with the present?

I want Gazi to have his own chapter in this book simply because I consider Gazi one of my best friends, with whom I have been able to share the good and the bad things of life for over 30 years. Gazi is special, due to his attitude and his drive to think and to plan 'big' as they say. He has always been inclined to undertake, to dare, to appreciate, and never waste time. He knows how to keep his friends and not lose them on the way. He has proven to be able to find the best in his friends and the people who surround him, so that they can move forward together with him.

In my eyes, Gazi is the prototype of the Albanian, who does not give up, but tries to be successful and an achiever in his own country. His endless desire to learn, to progress, as well as his practical way of making the best of any encounter have inspired me to move forward too. From our early days when we shared a school bench and followed private German language lessons at the house of Prof. Ignacio, Gazi always exerted a special influence over me.

Gazi talks mainly about achievements, projects, and challenges. He talks in these terms because that is how he has constructed his life. Our conversation at the Hotel Rogner was followed by a visit to the new offices of his company, 'The Albanian Experience' and then to his new house – a residential villa in the nearby hills surrounding Tirana. Everything is new, it radiates welfare and order, the way I wish to see all of Albania.

Here is Gazi's story:

I think very few Albanians live like I do, even though life has become globalised in Albania too. Today I'm here, tomorrow I'm somewhere else because my business activities bring me there. Our targets are here and abroad. Life happens in Albania, we converse in Albanian, eat Albanian food, but I don't think as an 'Albanian'. The day has Albanian traits as much as American ones, the staff work in two languages, and our office can operate anywhere in the world. Certainly I remain Albanian in my genes, because I value how we Albanians relate to each other, how we relate and respect our parents, the closeness we share, but at the same time the fact is that I don't tolerate my daughter, still a child, using makeup. Even more without asking my permission.

When friends and colleagues visit us from abroad in Albania, I take them to the cities outside of Tirana, so that they can see the 'real Albania'. Everyone can have a bad experience in Albania, but it's people like you and I who can make Albania a good and special experience. Through the guide *Tirana in Your Pocket* no. 9, which will be released shortly, I try to do this. I've invested in this publication from its inception and we update it frequently.

Frankly speaking, I think I carve my style wherever I'm. I try to inspire people so that they can follow me and not fear me. We talk and I train them, and when I ask: 'How do you feel compared to other young people of your age?' They answer: 'An altogether different experience'.

I don't use Facebook or Twitter to promote my business activities because I function very well without them. I feel I can be present where I want to be without the help of social media.

I consider myself lucky. Anila is my wife and best friend. She is a sophisticated woman, with both feet still on the ground. I rely on her, I consult her, I can discuss important issues with her and she also sits on the board of my company. There she doesn't operate as the wife of the chief, but independently, analysing everything accurately and courageously.

❖

These are times of change and expansion. The business is maturing. One project leads to another. We are actually the main partner for the Balkan Peninsula and are becoming the main player for this region for the Asian tourism market. We have 12 new buses, 405 new cars and several minibuses.

Another challenge has been getting the licenses for Avis and Budget. There is a lot of competition but we were first on the list. The chief director of Budget paid us a visit, after which we bought the license. We will be opening new offices in Kosovo, Macedonia and in Asia in the near future. We are also supporting a big project which includes the Greek company that was responsible for the construction of the Elbasan highway. They are interested in utilising our services in Macedonia.

It was a personal challenge for me to become the main partner in the Balkans for the Asian tourism market. 'Balkan' is a broad concept, because it starts from Moldova, continues to Romania, Bulgaria, Macedonia and Serbia. Our company takes care of everything. We send our buses to Moldova and from there to Serbia. We have changed the model of this business. Some three to four years ago, the Croats and the Slovenians would give us part of the business and would say: 'Here it is, if you want, you can take care of accommodation'. But now, by contacting the partners in Asia directly, we decide ourselves how to arrange things and who to trust our services to. For this reason, my colleague was in Hong Kong one month ago, I was in Taiwan last week, in September I will be in Japan, and in November in Hong Kong and Indonesia. Two of my colleagues are presently travelling in Singapore and Malaysia.

The second challenge is to consolidate all that we have achieved and to expand cautiously because we have plenty of opportunities. We also have a good reputation, and there is a great demand and I believe we have the muscle to afford the change and the expansion. We need to increase the staff, to train the personnel, old and new, in order to keep up and manage these new developments.

Nowadays I'm busy mainly with two things: promoting the strategy and the culture of the company. I spend a lot of time on the road taking care of this aspect of the business. Anila leads the day-to-day operations here in Albania. The spirit of change is felt in the office too. Migena is the chief of the finance department. Gjergji is in charge of banking, Tani deals with our 'special projects'. A new guy has just started as chief of operations at the 'Albanian Experience'. To start with, I sent him to follow a study at Bled, the Management School in Slovenia, where I teach. He's 28 years old. We paid for his studies and we didn't even have a contract obliging him to work with us upon completion. He however returned and has started working with us. The average age of the staff is between 29 and 40. We consult and confer with foreign mentors, and lecturers of the best universities in the world. We discuss with them business strategy and our options to expand or cut back when needed.

The latest development is the approval of an English MBA for the POLIS University. I would like to start there with an incubator of ideas, concerning all aspects of life and not particularly our business. For example, the idea to start a kindergarten, on the basis of a new concept, can be born there. What seems very interesting to me is that in one way or another the ideas and initiatives in one field relate and feed into other fields too.

Let me be precise. I see myself as a package and in perpetual change. When we are dining with friends, I try to talk about things that are not related to my work, because I have other interests too. A particular quality of mine is the fact that I feel responsible. I'm a family person. Relatives approach me when they are in trouble and in need. I take the time to understand what their problems are, as I take the time to explain to my mother how our business is going. We live together with my mum, who takes care of us. Most importantly she has a very good relationship with Anila. This makes me happy, because it motivates my mum to live and to be with us longer. I appreciate that she doesn't regard it a burden when she cooks or prepares breakfast for the whole family. I really try to give fair due to everything I do and to all the people around me.

I have a sense of achievement. I've clearly set my targets. My goal is not to start here and to end up there, the targets themselves are work in progress. The feeling of success makes me feel alive. The feeling of making things possible, things that matter for society as a whole, keeps me alive. This is because I do want to see myself as useful.

If you have a sense of what you want to achieve, setting targets becomes easier. For example, I personally feel I have to be modest, to continue to learn as well as try to get to the top of my profession. I've been invited to go at the end of October for a three-hour lecture at Tuck Business School. It is one of the best in the United States. I consider this a great honour and achievement. I believe that in the business world you absolutely can't function without objectives and targets.

Sometime ago I decided to lose weight – my target was about eight kilograms. It was a personal challenge and my intention was to realise the value of sports. I can safely say that I did achieve this goal.

Something else that comes to mind is that Anila and I have many close friends who live in Albania. I believe you can't have friends if you do not invest time in the friendship. I think we have achieved this and for me this is important – not only having colleagues and acquaintances, but having really close friends.

I would like to be a good and irreplaceable son, husband, brother and father. Indeed, I spend a lot of time on the road, but I know that here in Albania, I'm useful and needed.

I think life is a process. I'm not the same person I used to be one year ago, or three years ago for that matter. I often have wake-up calls, such as when I lost my niece. I had to think and consider many things. Often, at the end of a day or one of my trips, I get home to find Anila tired and thoughtful. Then I begin to reflect and ask myself if I'm not being too ambitious with my goals and all that I want to achieve. We have worked together all these years. And I want this to continue. So my conversations and discussions with Anila are also wake-up calls for me.

I was in secondary school, when I started learning English, and no other member of my family or relatives spoke any English. I could not understand a single word when our teacher Arta Dade spoke. I used to listen to 'Voice of America' on the radio and I still did not understand a single word. But I was determined to learn the English language, because for me it was 'either you make it or you break it'. This was a challenge. Another challenge was the university, where I wanted to graduate with the highest scores. My experience in America was another challenge. On the one hand I was the 'interesting' stoic Albanian, who was in need of funding so that he could study further, on the other hand I had to change, to adapt quickly, to become more open-minded. I remember I learned in America to wear short trousers and to get used to the idea of having two pairs of walking shoes, one for the summer and one for the winter, a $100 each. In those days I counted every penny.

The tendency to undertake and become an entrepreneur came naturally. Since my 16th birthday, I worked as a guide, with the few tourist groups that visited Albania then, to earn some money. When I started in Columbia University, I could survive thanks to income I earned from translating English and French. When in need, you get to learn and do many things. I was given these translation projects by the Soros Foundation in Albania. I was paid $4,000, which was for me a huge amount of money. I invited my parents to visit me in the States and I gave them $2,000 so they could renovate their bathroom, buy new chairs and repair their whole house.

I think it was during this period that I had fine-tuned my ambitions. I felt defined and was not in an identity crisis. Even now when I meet friends from my childhood I take the time to talk with them, because in my view nothing has changed in relation to them. Perhaps I have more money than they do, but it's not money that makes and defines me.

My decision to stay and to invest in Albania and not to migrate abroad has been my role and contribution to Albanian society. This is how I make sense of what I do.

A friend, who has been living and studying abroad, made a comment when he saw the new villa that we have built: 'I see that you have made such a big investment here, amid this filth. This house in New York would be worth 20 million. Don't you regret the investment? My answer to that was: 'This filth is good for us, because we have decided to live and change things here.'

I've chosen to distance myself from politics. Clinically distant. Really distant. My business is not dependent on politics and politics can't exploit me. I have friends and acquaintances in all walks of life and this has only a good and positive influence on my business, but at the same time it keeps me independent. I follow my own politics and do not engage in politics.

Certainly I do exploit my connections with politicians and all the possibilities that are at my disposal. I use my contacts, but nowadays it's the politicians that need me. Our company offers the best services in our field in the whole country. For example, we have a multi-year contract with UNICEF for the organisation of their events the coming years, and we have also started working closely with the European Union.

We did not have to pay to start POLIS University, nor for the license for the English MBA that was approved a few days ago. We had to discuss, argue and clarify our position and request. We spoke with some key people in the sector. We certainly have our own lobby.

In the end we succeeded and the officials of the Ministry

of Education said it was an honour to work with us.

Understand me. I make my money abroad. My money comes from abroad. Our income is mainly generated there. What can Albanian politicians do to Taiwanese tourists, who arrive in groups? I have diversified the risk. This is a choice. I have spent many sleepless nights thinking about this. My intention is to build a business I can be proud of. That needs guts. And I have relayed this spirit to my team which works hard and takes care of the business in my absence. When I started with the tourist business, some said: 'What a stupid thing to do – to go and get them from Moldova'. I said: 'Let's try'. Now in one day we get 18 tour groups, who mainly come from Asia, but also from Europe. They arrive here and we make the big Balkan tour possible for them.

I have been lucky with the parents I have. I wouldn't have wanted other parents. If they had been better educated and more inclined to open doors for me – I would have had an easier start. But I'm very happy with what they have given me through the years. My entire family has been a great support, to me, to us, and my mother continues to help and take care of us today.

My parents taught me that life has no short-cuts. You have to work to get somewhere. Another lesson has been: 'Dare and face life! If there is something which doesn't go well, face it and work on it. Otherwise do not demand anything, just sleeping and waiting for things to fall from the sky is not an option'.

Everyone leads his or her own life. It is not up to me to judge others and their decisions. I'm Gazi from Albania, who does well in his country. If I would be Gazi from America I would have created a different profile, and not been the one I am now.

I think it's important to show to the Albanian generation that has been brought up abroad what Albania has to offer. I don't believe in loving your fatherland, but I do believe in finding yourself and opportunities in this reality. I don't think that those who left the country and have lived for 25 years abroad should come back. They and their children could come back only if they find possibilities and opportunities to grow here.

My family is from Chameria, an Albanian region of the Balkans under Greek control. For me, the Cham question is important mainly from a philosophical point of view, because I have not been born and do not have any roots there. It matters because I honour the feelings of my parents and my grandparents, who were expelled from their own land. It also matters because we do justice by recognising that the denial of the Cham question is an historic injustice in itself. On a philosophical level everything is emotionally charged. The material aspect is not important. It has no real value. I'm the Chair of the Institute of Chameria. Tomorrow we are going to Sarande, where we have organised a summer school where the Cham question will be discussed and popularised. I'm very serious about these issues, though I realise that the Cham question will not be resolved unless it makes it to the agenda of Europe or America. I don't want the Cham question to die out and that's why we are publishing and promoting books about it. We just had a book promoted in England. We are also organising events such as the latest performance of the State Ensemble with songs and dances from Chameria.

I'm for an Albania without borders, because borders are artificially created. They mean isolation and chasms. I don't think that the Balkan Peninsula is a dangerous region, though it's called the powder keg. An economically developed Balkans doesn't need borders.

Thinking about Albania 20 years from now, I imagine it like Italy, Greece or Spain – at their best version. With people who travel, who study, who return, with multicultural marriages. An open society.

In Albania we need to strengthen our sense of responsibility. The biggest problem here is that people have expectations from others. People have to learn to take responsibility for themselves, their own lives and their own futures. Related to the business world: we need to organise, to support each other, to lobby better in favour of the economic development of the country.

I want to be around for a long time. I want to enjoy my achievements, my family, my children. I have two personal objectives: to brush up my German and my French. I certainly think in the long term about my children. My daughter Sibora has told me she wants to follow in my footsteps and she already speaks English very well.

I could have done some things differently. Other things I will still do in the same way again. I'm happy with what I have. I have no anger. My life under communism, like all Albanians, was defined by the system. I think I've got other things from that regime, which in one way or the other have kept people near each other. When they finished working, people used to enjoy themselves in their own way, intensively. The quality and the intensity of the human relations and family relations of those times have to be valued.

Many great friendships were born then. Just recall the two of us going for the German lessons. In those days children used to play outdoors without fear, the world was a less dangerous place for them, whereas today my mum keeps watching them from the balcony if they go outside on their own. Because we have so much more to lose, don't we?

Birds of a feather flock together

In my eyes my parents were young when they got married. In the same period that I was born, my mother graduated from the university. She looks at the camera thoughtfully, in a white wedding dress, next to my father, surrounded by friends and with me in her belly. I try to grasp from her gaze if she really understood what was happening to them and to what extent she desired me. The shutter of the camera had clicked several times during that evening. In another photo, she smiles. It feels as if her clear gaze reaches further ahead in time, in the future and finds me here writing about them. How young they were – I think for the thousandth time, and I try to recall them as they were then : light, strong, positive and programmed to survive.

As with many other things, they fed me with the idea that friendship is a wonderful and a special phenomenon. They both have many friends, who have accompanied them wherever they have been. Even nowadays, retired and not engaged with politics or business, the first thing my parents do when they visit my sister in the United States or me in the Netherlands is update the contact details of their friends, who are now spread all over the world. And returning home to Tirana is more than anything else a return to their friends. Though it takes some days before they again get used to the small and crowded apartment where they live, climbing up to the fifth floor, to the perforating voice of the TV presenters, they need just an hour to connect with their friends and make appointments. In fact, some of these appointments are made even before they take the return journey. So once back home there is nothing else to do but to flow with the stream.

However, what has most attracted and affected me in putting friendship on a pedestal and giving it a very special status is not the harmony that it brought to our family, but something else, not easily defined, almost indispensable and somehow problematic and unexplainable. I think this relates to the combative spirit of my father. Though he is known to be a wise man, on the home front he was possessed by a fighting spirit. During the first years of their coexistence and my childhood, and maybe even nowadays, they perceived their friends as amplifiers that strengthened their individuality and prevented them from melting and harmonising with each other. On many occasions when my parents would talk or argue about things, they would draw in the names of each other's friends. Why did my father perceive as a hindrance some special qualities of my mother and her friends? And why did my mother not withhold herself, but retaliate by referring to friends of my father as being uncontrollable and uninhibited? What prevented them from giving in, and surrendering to each other? Was it to assert their influence only, their invisible long hand? Was it to remain solid individuals? Was it an attempt not to be 'average' and to challenge 'the norm' that gave them so much strength to persevere in this pattern, which I so often experienced as suffocating?

In my eyes, their friends would get the status of dissidents, because each time they would not agree about this or that, their stubbornness at that point was somehow recognised as a feature they shared with their respective friends, who would attract them like magnets and strengthen their individuality and undermine their unity. So I grew up with the idea that friends first and foremost helped them to keep their individuality alive. Striving to be and remain an individual in a patriarchal society, which recognised orders and radiated only unity, where the (class) enemy was permanently invented, required strong nerves and persistence.

The friends I refer to here include all their friends: from their childhood, their youth, their university days, colleagues; and friends from their jobs at radio Tirana, at the newspapers, the many schools my mother taught at, friends made during their military training, friends with whom my father shared his passion for painting and for playing billiards, as well as the neighbours with whom my mum takes her morning coffee. All of them have been mentioned in one way or another in these conversations, which were often explosive due to my parent's particularities and difference of opinions. All have been 'accomplices' in my parents' refusal to bend to each other.

But as time went by, the friends of one became the friends of both and it looked as if my parents had become less thirsty for struggles and more flexible, even more so because together they could better face the external pressures and many challenges of life, and ultimately for us, their two daughters who were growing up and questioning their authority. I, no longer alarmed by their high-pitched voices, could better distinguish the sub-tones of their conversations and all that was not being said but were as important, and so I would understand that their world and my world was luckily full of colours and not only black and white. It was their friends, among others, who broke the light into colours and made life worth living and more valuable. So friendship under dictatorship was very valuable, because it helped the individual to stand up to the many pressures, including the forged family unity where difference of opinion was not allowed.

According to the poet and academic C.S. Lewis: 'Friendship is unnecessary, like philosophy, like art... It has no survival value; rather it's one of those things which gives value to survival.' C.S. Lewis was a close friend of J.R.R. Tolkien, known for his fantasy novels The Hobbit and The Lord of the Rings. Tolkien is thought to be the father of the fantastic literature. If I continue thinking in this line, does not friendship have some fantastic elements? How often did I dream of having a pen friend in the old days, when connecting with the outer world was forbidden in Albania? How often have I dreamt, and have embodied my friends with almost extra-terrestrial qualities? And how much do I like the Albanian proverb that says 'find your friends better than yourself'? This requires the capacity to recognise yourself, to accept yourself the way you are, including the imperfections and defects, as well as the wisdom in making choices.

My parents have gathered around them many friends, all with

their virtues and vices, passions and issues, some known for their sense of humour, some for their intelligence, some for their problems, some for their non-conflicting spirits, ability to be at ease, and generosity, all with their own stories. To my knowledge, none of these friends has let them down and their friendships have endured the many tests of the old days, when any effort to be different, to move up or down, to go right or left, to think or compose differently, to speak or to write differently, even to be dressed differently was punished. Many have been wounded and hurt because of their desire to be different. That is why for me nurturing friendships during the dictatorship did have a survival value in itself. Friendship was the oxygen that cleared the soul that did not want to surrender and to weaken.

The conversations that went on until late at night around the little kitchen table at our house, during the holidays at the coast, walking along the sidewalks of the boulevard 'Martyrs of the Nation', sitting on the parapets of Rinia park, and at some smoke-filled cafes are unrepeatable and unforgettable as long as we, the witnesses are alive.

Greta

> *Without music life would have been a mistake.*
> Friedrich Nietzsche: *Twilight of the Idols*

Not every word finds its place adequately in a spoken sentence, within a poem or a text. Not every note finds its place in a piece of music, even more so when it has to fit with other notes and with a word. The same goes for people. Not all of us manage to fit into and feel realised within a certain group, a generation, a given community or society, even more so if the rules of that society or community are predetermined and dictatorial, gravely limiting opportunities for personal expression and development. An individual's reaction to a set of rules is quite personal. Soon enough something will happen because the individual's desire for meaning and control over his or her existence is as old as being.

Teta *Greta was my first music teacher*[3]. *With the G major key, she opened the gate to a world without limits for many children of my generation – the world of music. You may recall that American scientists included a collection of Voyager Golden Records on board the Voyager spacecraft in 1977. The phonograph records contained music and images of our planet and were intended for any intelligent extraterrestrial life or future humans who may come across them. According to Carl Sagan, the records resembled a 'bottle' launched into the 'cosmic ocean' and were a very hopeful statement about life on this planet. In a similar way, at the same time in the little town of Kruja, Greta Mullaj, my music teacher, threw her message into the ocean of her pupil's feelings. Trying to communicate with us through music, she ignored the many fences, divisions and security measures that beset us, as well as her own exclusion, the physical and spiritual isolation that the communist regime had forced upon her. It seems strange now to observe that as a music teacher she was maltreated, to say the least.*

Teta Greta was for me the most beautiful teacher on earth, with her elegant figure, her wavy hair hiding her small forehead, the smooth skin of her cheeks, her beautiful lips, hands that played her instrument or conducted above our heads, and twinkling eyes that observed, translated and spoke of beautiful worlds filled with music, even when her lips became tight and did not produce a sound. She was like the fairy-tale beauty Snow White, who worked so hard, so unquestioningly, at her menial tasks, attracting everyone with her grace and wisdom, while all the time she was a gifted princess with no inkling of who she was or where she came from.

Greta's love for children merged with her love of music and made her shine, inspiring us and awakening in us the same passion for music she had. Her gracious manner and her pleasant personality gave her a special place in our hearts. She was a simple teacher of music who, thanks to the mercy or, rather, the reduced vigilance of those who governed so-called 'class enemies' at that time, was allowed to teach at an elementary school in a small town like Kruja. The order from above had lost something of its imperative along the way. She was not deported to work on a collective farm, as were many people who were 'affected' and who were seen as suspicious, anti-revolutionary and potentially dangerous. If not persecuted or eliminated they were effectively removed from community life, forced to work in the fields from morning until evening to ensure their survival.

Those men who ruled us on behalf of the Communist Party – I say 'men' because most of them were healthy blockheads – had no idea of the power of music or its impact on the minds and hearts of children. They did not know how Teta Greta's influence penetrated the closed circles of Kruja's family groups. She had made herself almost invisible, remaining always in the shadow, never loudly praised or encouraged in public, but in possession of a secret skill that made her one with her music, communicating through it news of another world – a bigger, better, freer and more beautiful world. This is the strength of art, surpassing the power of mortal rulers.

Years have passed by. This record of a morning conversation with

Teta Greta in a sunny café on the Adriatic coast is an effort to share with you the life of a very dear person who suffered and struggled but also experienced great joy through her passion for music and for teaching others how to feel and enjoy it, in the process making them better and more complete people. Let us start with the music:

When I was 6 years old, my mother, who was a young woman with three children and many challenges facing her, met Bardha Prodani, a good friend who had learned about a new boarding school which had just opened in Tirana, the Artistic Lyceum. 'Children live there, they study and become musicians. If you want, we can arrange for Greta to be admitted,' she suggested. And so it happened. It was December, the school year had begun in September, and I was the youngest in my class. The others had already learned the alphabet. My mum chose the violin as my instrument.

To tell you the truth, what I really wanted to do was play with other children in the street. I was swift and restless and full of energy, so the teachers found little tasks for me to do. 'Greta, can you fetch the firewood?', 'Greta do this, Greta do that!' Professor Paparisto was my tutor. Apparently they thought I had talent although I didn't study much. Six months after I started learning to play the violin a big concert was organised. Representatives of the government, the Communist Party and many foreigners attended. It was 1955. In spite of the many difficulties my family experienced, my mum didn't want us to feel the absence of our father who, as I vaguely understood it, was abroad, so she donated blood to earn money to buy me a white pair of sandals and a piece of Chinese silk taffeta. She brought the cloth to Ada, a very good tailor who made it up for me. In that dress I looked like a butterfly. I remember I played two little pieces of Mozart and Mendelssohn.

In 1957 my mother was expelled from the Communist Party. My father, Major Galip Sojli, who until then had been praised and trusted by the party, was declared an enemy. My father had been sent abroad by the Albanian Intelligence Service. He was caught and forced, most probably under torture, to become a double agent. His 'betrayal' cast a shadow over our lives. As a child I didn't understand what had happened. From then on my family and I experienced only trouble. At school they had to consult with party officials before I was allowed to appear at a concert.

My passion for the violin and my inextricable link with the instrument started with an ugly incident at the Lyceum. I was 12 years old. Some high-level party members visited the school. My class friends were playing and, among other mishaps, they tore some of the classroom wall posters which were full of news, directives and achievements of the school. I had not joined in the rowdy play. I knew my place. But someone had to be blamed for this act. The school council decided that it was my fault and I was expelled. Even now I don't know if the whole thing was set up. Perhaps the torn posters were simply an excuse. In any case it was a blow that hurt a good deal.

My mother left no stone unturned and finally found me a violin teacher for private lessons. For me he was not simply a music teacher, nor was his family a family like all others. They became my guardian angels for all the years that followed. Both husband and wife, Islam (Lam) Petrela and Vasilika Petrela, became my teachers, my mentors and, in one way, my parents as well. They spent hours educating me and developing all my skills. I owe my musical development to them. In those days they used to live in a basement because Lam was 'persecuted'. Later, as far as I know, due to the work of Vasilika's father, they were able to move to a simple apartment. At their place I started listening to music for hours, reading everything I could lay my hands on, day and night. My daily regime changed completely. They were both excellent teachers who made me love the instrument and taught me self-discipline. I would stay until late at night at their place, sometimes until 11pm. I probably did not have a good posture, but Lam prompted me to practice for 7 or 8 hours a day. Every day I started at 5 am. The violin became my life. Everything, every joy, every sorrow, all my feelings and my love for the world I tried to express through the violin. Certainly I loved people, but I laughed, cried and lived through my violin. I realised the violin would open a way for me. It would make me become visible, become someone.

After many attempts, my mother managed to enrol me again at the Lyceum. At the age of 18 I graduated with grade 10. Of course it was not a simple matter to award the highest grade to the daughter of Galip Sojli, who remained an enemy. Although I had achieved the highest grade, I was not granted the right to continue my studies at the Conservatorium, nor at any other faculty. I was immediately appointed a school teacher in Gramsh instead. Gramsh was known as a town where internally displaced families were sent. I had to experience Gramsh alone.

I suffered a lot in those days. I don't know how to express it in words. What could I do? You can't bang your head against a brick wall. I was only 18 years old. My salvation during this crisis, when I was really hurt by the official dictat, was once again the violin. I continued practicing and playing nonstop.

❀

Shortly after I went to Gramsh, I was invited to join a folk orchestra, although I didn't have any particular affection for folk music. I understood then that the only way to feel connected to music and to feel useful was to teach. I put together a chorus of 120 children. Into every musical note of that choir I put my heart. In that small town, people were friendly and spoke well of me, especially the older women who were considerate and sympathetic, perhaps because, despite my young age, I tried to behave like a mature woman. Out of necessity I had matured. Their good words restored my trust and gave me confidence in what I was doing.

I was form teacher to a class at the school, so I started working seriously with them. There were 40 pupils, each one poorer than the next. I remember one boy, Jakup, who was 10 years old with a big head and blue eyes. He was an orphan who had no family so he lived with the woodcutters on the mountain. I approached the chief of the education section in order to arrange for Jakup to board nearby so he could attend school more regularly. It worked. He came to school regularly, finished elementary school, and his life became easier compared with others growing up alone in the forest.

In Gramsh, I kept myself busy preparing for concerts and children's choir performances. I worked long hours so we could give several concerts a year: on national holidays such as 28-29 November, New Year's Eve, 1 May, etc.

I continued doing this in Kruja, where I went to work after Gramsh. I went there with Rrezi, my husband. We lived 20 years in Kruja. During those years, the children's choirs won the flag three times in children's festivals throughout the district. That meant we were considered the best of the school choirs from Laç, Fushe, Kruja, Thumana and other residential centres in the district. In addition, the children's choir of Kruja won three national awards. It meant a lot to me, and it was accomplished through the hard work of all the children. I had a great feeling of pleasure and satisfaction in it. My work and my achievement with these children's choirs offset the lack of any direct appreciation for my skills and talents as a violin player, which is why, in those years, all my passion for the violin was transformed into a passion for teaching. I liked the songs composed in those days, full of love – for the mother, the homeland, the martyrs, for each other. Despite the fact that very often the leading cadres didn't trust my commitment or didn't appreciate my work – they even tried to keep me from the stage, forcing me to play the violin behind curtains – I considered teaching my duty.

Albania was my country, and my pupils were the children of the town where my own children were growing up. I taught them the ABC of singing and I had a friendly relationship with many of the parents.

In Kruja, I founded a group of violinists. We strived for quality, regardless of the fact that some of the parents were a little obstructive and uncommitted. It was different from Gramsh where many families had been forced to transfer from all over the country; in Kruja, people proved to be more open-minded about the music and the singing.

Looking back, I can say that I really felt good wherever I worked, although the children and their parents often did not understand that you have to make sacrifices in order to learn to play an instrument. In a way it was understandable – I didn't teach in a professional music school and many of the parents did not have great musical ambitions for their children. I'm totally convinced that our music schools in those days were good.

❧

My life was not easy, but I never lost my perspective. Rrezi and I did not meet at a concert though we both loved and played music. In Kruja, Rrezi helped me a lot by accompanying the violin with his accordion during the children's choir rehearsals, but when we met, I didn't know that he played the accordion. We met at a party organised by my cousin. I was a teenager, Rrezi was a bit older, he was 19 then. After that we used to greet each other in the street. He had very good manners, unusually traditional for those revolutionary days. His grandfather was ill so I used to ask about him. My cousin thought the two of us would make a perfect match. So the years went by and I grew up. One day Rrezi asked me if he could treat me to a pastry. He had just graduated from university.

We went together to a patisserie where there used to be some very good pastries you could get for 15 leks. Until that day I had never entered a patisserie on my own. It may seem surprising, but with Lika (Vasilika Petrela) I had a very conservative education. She set a standard of perfection for everything we did. Life had probably taught them *fin troppo* to be polite, reserved and moderate in expression, whereas my mother was the opposite – of them and of me. Even now she is ninety she still likes to dance, to sing, to laugh, to have fun. I really do not take after her at all. When my parents were young they enjoyed life and went dancing whenever they could, whereas Lika was so particular and so controlled that she did not even allow me to attend my diploma celebration. I submitted to her. She wanted me to become 'someone', at all costs, and the price was that I could not behave like the others, but had to show maturity and wisdom. For good or bad, this is how I was brought up during those absurd times.

My relationship with Rrezi continued and after my three years in Gramsh we decided to get married and went to work together in Kruja. Rrezi's support through all these years has been invaluable. He is sweet, humane, well-educated and comes from a very cultured family. Maybe I was not as lucky in my life, considering my relationship with the violin, but God gave me a wonderful family. My family and Rrezi's family have been my good fortune, and they have compensated for my unrealised dream of becoming a famous violin player.

Now I'm 67 years old and I've been working for 49 years. For me, work is the most important thing in life, whether it's singing with paralysed old ladies, giving music lessons at school, directing the children's choirs, directing the violin ensemble or, as I do nowadays, teaching students in Italy.

What gave meaning to my life and made me feel fulfilled is the fact that my daughter Suela became a violinist. She was also prevented from entering the Artistic Lyceum. It was 1981 and she was 6 years old then. We were living in Kruja. When she went to register for the entrance competition, she wasn't allowed to. I know humans are able to endure a lot of pain, but when you witness your own child being excluded, it hurts you even more than your own exclusion. The people in power were simply malicious. Rrezi arranged for a meeting with Xhemal Dymylja, the first secretary of the Party Committee in Kruja, and begged him to help so that Suela could register for the competition. He did help us and she was given the right to enter. She won the competition and was able to attend the Lyceum.

It was a new challenge, a hope, a joy. In those days, I went to Tirana every day after school, worked with Suela for 3-4 hours and then returned back home to Kruja. It was really an exhausting experience, with bad transport connections, overloaded buses and long working hours at school. But I invested all the time I had in her and it was an extraordinary pleasure because Suela had talent.

When she plays a violin solo I feel as if my soul is in her. I feel as if I'm one with her, as if I'm playing too. The first time this happened I was surprised, I could not really understand what was happening, but music can make this happen. It recognises no age, no boundaries, no ideologies. An artist on stage doesn't belong to herself, she is part of the universal harmony.

When Suela started attending the Lyceum, she was taught by Robert Papavrami, who has done so much for the establishment of the Albanian violin school. Berti has supported us a lot. He was courageous. He and Zhani Ciko really contributed to Suela's education at the Lyceum, helping her to develop as a professional, even though she was a child.

As the years went by, Suela proved to have more musical intuition and she had a better musical education than I did. She has matured as an instrumentalist under very different circumstances from me. Fate reserved Kruja and Gramsh for me, whereas Suela, has been able to live a free life from the age of 15. She could travel abroad and has had lessons from very well-regarded and famous professors.

The nineties, as the beginning of another era, brought huge changes to our lives. This is how we experienced the events at the beginning: One night, in the early hours, we heard people talking loudly and singing *For the Motherland* and other partisan songs in the street. Our house was near Elbasani road, not far from the Students' Town. I was with Lule, Rrezi's sister, and as we listened behind the big door of the courtyard, we whispered to each other: Are we in a dream? Is this really happening? For decades Tirana had not experienced any spontaneous demonstration or protest. In the morning, without waiting any longer, we went to the Students' Town and could feel the times were changing. That day I felt in my bones what it meant to be free.

We had killed the fear. They were really extraordinary days. I could feel a new world opening up in front of us. Time went by. From the 'invasion' of the embassies to the ships in Durres, it all felt as if I was living a dream that I had waited for all my life. Our son, Mili, wanted to leave the country at all costs. He tried and tried, at first unsuccessfully via the Hungarian forests during the winter, then by boat. Finally, he reached Austria by plane. He had courage, while we – his parents and his grandparents – watched with great concern. He was not alone. Thousands of his generation wanted to leave – often hungry, often like vagabonds, all needy, all of them in search of a better life. In search of freedom.

The changes were irreversible. Zhani Ciko created a group with some young musicians, and Suela was one of them. But even in those last days, when the dictatorship was gasping its last breath, Suela had a very unpleasant experience. The group was preparing to go and perform in Greece. At the very last moment, we were told that Suela could not join the group. She was only 14 years and yet she could not be spared because she was my daughter and the granddaughter of Galip Sojli. This happened in 1990, just a few months before the regime fell. The rest of the group went to Greece while she stayed behind. They really wanted to break her, as they had tried with me, in a very systematic way. I know Zhani Ciko tried his best to take her, but with no success. Some months later, the group was invited to perform in Austria. This time Suela could go. It gave her so much confidence and self-esteem. Upon her return from Austria, we started looking for music competitions in neighbouring countries, and we found one in Gorizia. Suela's teacher was Roland Xhoxhi, who was a very good mentor to her. Suela prepared and we went. A new chapter of our lives began, a life full of unknowns and adventures, for us both, mother and daughter. I was 42 years, Suela 15.

We had only $100 and around 50,000 lire on us. We travelled by ferry from Durrës to Trieste for 26 hours. Suela's professor came with us. On the ship, Suela became friends with an Italian trader. She spoke good Italian and could tell him about her life. Suela is different from me. Even to this day I'm still reserved. The Italian trader was called Antonio Bernardi and he said: 'Listen, my daughter, if you need help, just call and I will be there for you'. This encounter was lucky for us. The first immigrants who 'stormed' Italy from Albania were received willingly by good people, simple people, as well as by the state. They were generously helped and accommodated, unlike the experience of the last few years.

I think it's us Albanians who should be blamed for the Italians' change of attitude, because we often behave in embarrassing ways, defying the law and values of Italian society. We went to Gorizia. Our new Italian friend arranged accommodation for us and mobilised other people who were willing to help us as well. We stayed a couple of days there. Suela won a prize at the competition but everything was complicated and very expensive. We had only our dreams and an iron will to succeed at any cost. I'm very grateful to all those who helped us move forward along new and unknown paths in Italy. We have lived in Italy for many years now. My family and I all feel very good here, in our second home, and I can wholeheartedly say that I feel endless gratitude and love for the Italians. We have never felt like foreigners or suffered exclusion in Italy. Instead, I've felt honoured and valued.

Suela competed in Sondra too. She won a second prize

there and this helped financially. After some months Suela entered the competition at the Giuseppe Verdi Conservatory and won a place. She graduated *cum laude*.

We were befriended and very much supported at this time by a Catholic priest, who was a friend of the Italian trader Bernardi. He met us at the station and arranged temporary accommodation for us. He also organised a concert in his church. Suela played the violin beautifully. Being so young and coming from Albania she really impressed the audience. Hard-working children are rare in Italy. There is a welfare system, so children are supported and do not have to make sacrifices, whereas in Albania I remember children learning to play instruments in schools without windows, in classrooms without heating, with hands swollen from the cold, for six to seven hours a day. When the concert ended, Suela said, 'I would like to say few words about Albania'. She managed to tell the story of her country in Italian, with pain and pride at the same time. She mentioned all the wonderful people she had known in her homeland, their desire to be free and to live with dignity, and she talked about the regime that had destroyed the lives of so many families for decades. My heart swelled with each word of hers. Children grow up and we are surprised by their strength and their will.

A new life started for me too. It wasn't easy, for we were two women who often didn't know where we would sleep at night or where we were going the next day. You can't survive on freedom alone. Even less with only dreams to sustain you. But I was prepared to endure and even enjoy the insecurity that freedom gave us. Not only for Suela and myself, but for our whole family. Rrezi had remained behind in Albania.

Suela entered the conservatory in January. In June she played Sibelius with the RAI orchestra, and there in the hall

I saw two thousand people applauding. It was a beautiful thing, very touching. At the Conservatory Suela was befriended by another violinist whose name was Francesca. Franscesca and her family also supported us at that time. She lent Suela a very good violin and her family helped me to find work. After one year of wandering through Italy, I started working at a music academy in Campo Basso, a town quite far from Milan, where we had settled. I taught there as the assistant of well-known *maestros* such as Giles and Vernikov.

There my life as a recognised violin teacher began. I was able to realise my lifelong dream, denied to me in my own country. Working in the postgraduate academy was a great responsibility, considering that I had never formally finished my musical education. I trusted myself and, with courage, I succeeded. I felt I was becoming more accomplished with each day, and once again I was using all my skills to teach students how to improve their posture, how to maintain the rhythm, how to work with the sound and correct their shortcomings. It was a demanding job, teaching four to five hours a day, going by train up and down to Milan, but it was the first time in my life that I was doing what I had always wanted to do, so I was as happy as a child. I was teaching music students.

After nearly two years, I started working in another academy closer to Milan, teaching children. Most importantly, I began to study the violin myself again, for many hours a day, because I was convinced that only hard work could bring us success in Italy. I must confess that I can hardly go one day without practicing and teaching. I feel like a permanent student.

For the past decade I've played very well. A friend of Suela's, who is always searching for old instruments, gave us a violin made by Giovanni Francesco Pressenda, who studied at the School of Cremona and is recognised as one of the best violin makers of the Turin school in the early eighteenth century. My violin has a reddish colour and makes you feel the colour of the sound. Suela played it first and thought that it would be a good instrument for me. Indeed, an artist reflects herself and expresses her individuality through her instrument, that is to say that each of us leaves a sign in the 'harmonious table'. A song or a musical piece belongs to its time, and after some years it may lose its brilliance. It is the artist who gives new life to both a piece of music and to the instrument he or she plays, at the same time realising themselves in the process.

It is worth mentioning that for more than ten years now I've been working to establish a good class of violinists, ranging in age from 6 to 35 years. I've been working with some of them for many years now. Some have since been admitted to the conservatory and passed their grade 10 exams. They are all good, without exception. Together with Suela I've created a violin group, which is now a very good and well appreciated orchestra. It functions like a private school, and I teach there. The orchestra is called the United Europe Chamber Orchestra and is composed of professional musicians of Italian, French, German, Austrian, Polish, Russian, Albanian and Greek origin.

I've also given concerts together with Suela, for example, Bach for two violins, Vivaldi for two violins. They really go well. I'm very fond of Bach and I like Vivaldi too. Perhaps what I'm doing is nothing extraordinary, but still for me it's very important.

For six years Rrezi and I were separated. He stayed in Albania while I was in Italy with Suela. My return to the violin and Suela's education in Italy demanded commitment and sacrifice. Now I come back to Albania every month. I love my country, I love my people here, although in Italy I feel recognised and accomplished in my profession. My entire life is connected to my students and the violin.

※

I don't look back to my past life. I've had enough of envy, jealousy, the ignorance of those who saw me as the class enemy, those who did me harm. If I have any regrets, they concern my father. I was not kind to him. When he returned to Albania of his own free will and was imprisoned, I went only once to see him in prison. I had started my own family, so I tried to do everything to protect them. I didn't want to confront them with the terrible abyss of the state's paranoia. Even when my father was released from prison, I kept my distance. The day he was released, I was there, watching him from a distance. I didn't make a sign or say one word. The released prisoners were marching in step down the main street. I hid behind the onlookers, afraid that my father would see me and wave to me and everyone would learn who I was. It was painful and absurd.

Later on, when my father listened to me playing the violin he would cry. He had an artist's nature. His mother was Austrian, he was well read, spoke seven languages and had a glorious past as a partisan, together with my mother. What can I say? He fulfilled his duty when he went abroad, but he was caught, tortured, and could not resist. He willingly came back to Albania because he wanted to die in his own country. The moment he disembarked from the plane, he was handcuffed. He spent a long time in prison. I believe he once said to my mother that he deeply regretted that because of him I could not become somebody. When he was released from prison, he lived with my mother and Mali, my brother, and his family, in a one-room apartment, with a kitchen of 3x3 metres.

When they declared my father an enemy, they also sent my uncle to a labour camp, and they expelled my mother from the Communist Party, but she was strong and courageous and raised three children. She had to sacrifice much but I never saw her commit an error or lose her way. She was a nurse in a psychiatric hospital, then in a children's hospital, then in a polyclinic, working shifts, caring for patients as well as for us at home. I'm convinced that we, her children, became good and honest thanks to her. In those years, she donated blood hundreds of times in order to make both ends meet. It was not an easy life. My parents met as high school students, 15 and 16 years old. Both took to the mountains to fight as partisans against the fascists. Their love survived the war and then, later, a long separation. Fifteen years of no communication, no letters, no news. In our family, there was love. My grandmother played an important role in keeping the family together. She was Austrian but considered herself Albanian. She nurtured a love for classical music and often listened to Schubert and Strauss, because she had studied the piano as well as finance. My grandfather was a good quiet man. He graduated in economics in Austria where he met my grandma who was also a student. I learned good manners from my grandparents and an appreciation of delicacy.

I don't have great regrets. Perhaps I should have pleased my father more. My sister and my brother were closer to him. Maybe I was reserved, withdrawn or even a coward. Maybe I felt responsible for my new family. My father understood and respected my distance, and he did not consider it as indifference and coldness, but he did suffer from me keeping my distance.

Even if God doesn't exist, man needs God and the spiritual support for his actions which God offers. If I think about some of the events in my life, some particular situations make me think that God exists. Every person is born with his or her own destiny. For example, I've never felt drowned or lost, I've always tried to lead my life, convinced that I will be able to find a path, a way through.

I love people. I've always valued them for what they do and who they are. I've never spent much time with ignorant, talkative or harmful people. I avoid them like the plague. I identify with close friends like Liliana, Mita and Dhurata, the ones who were there for me in the difficult moments of my life. You have to understand that in the old days I could not even be photographed. Once, the director of the Cultural House of Kruja, during one of the children's festivals, said 'Greta, you have to stand behind the others and not at the front. There, behind the brass instruments'. 'What is this new formation of the orchestra where the violins are at the back?' I said desperately. I feel embarrassed each time I recall this kind of situation, not for what they did to me but for the poor people who had to act like this, either out of servility or sectarianism, in order to maintain their position.

Today, even though I'm no longer young, I still work and have little time to sleep. I'm not a heroine but every day must be well prepared to teach. I try to follow what is happening around me on the Internet.

I have no time to lose. The few friends that I have are truthful and are there for me. That's important.

I like only classical music. Many things have changed in Albania. Nowadays few people are really fond of classical music. I think our old orchestras were far better than the hundreds of orchestras that exist today, although there are still many good artists, violinists, pianists and singers who perform very well in Albania and abroad. But these are individuals. During the communist years, a school, a tradition was created. I'm not sure whether we are doing the right thing in the field of music today in Albania. I love my country but I'm afraid we are not taking the right steps. This has less to do with limited resources than with something else which I can't easily define. It could be that at the root of this absence of real and significant change is the inherited backwardness of the country.

Clara, my granddaughter, often listens to commercial music, though we have beautiful songs for children, with simple music – beautiful lullabies, songs of our composers – which can be sung and played by children themselves. A taste and an ear for music, and classical music in particular, has to be nourished at kindergarten age, starting with Brahms and his many beautiful simple melodies. A feeling for and enjoyment of music starts with our educators, who should be educated themselves and not simply be taken from the street. In educating a child to play and to love an instrument, you are aware that he or she will probably not become a musician, but what he or she will learn from this process is a passion for music, a sense of control and discipline as well as good posture. Our capacity to feel music and to connect with each other through music is what remains. In my view that's life itself.

Blandi

Happy is the man, who can make a living by his hobby.
George Bernard Shaw: *Pygmalion*

I do not have a brother. Had I had one, I would have liked him to be like my friend Blandi. I say this because I think that if I had been born a boy, it is very possible that I would have been like him. After all, we try to choose our friends similar to ourselves. If it is possible, and we know how, we choose them even better than ourselves.

I have known Blandi since we were fourteen. Like me, he came from the province to Tirana, and we started going to the International Secondary School of Foreign Languages 'Asim Vokshi', where we both followed the English stream. He came from the small town of Pogradec, on the shores of Lake Ohrid, I from the mountainous Kruja. Neither of us talked the way they did in Tirana. I fired away in the Kruja dialect, and Blandi did the same in Pogradec. In Tirana, they had their own 'tirona' style of talking. He was wearing a rose-coloured shirt with long sleeves on the first day he came to school. I still remember this, because he wore it all through high school, and on prom night, too. He was always neat and well-groomed, a thing which made my Grandma (may she rest in peace) say to me: 'I like this boy, because he is white like porcelain', and then she would wink at me. I guess she knew that he was Mario Ashiku's son, a very well-known actor in her days, and undoubtedly one of the most handsome men in Albania in the fifties and sixties.

We lived in the same neighbourhood, practically on the same street, and in those years we would relentlessly roam the streets of Tirana in every season, rain or shine. On occasion, we skipped school together, and went to the movies and cafés, watched video films and listened to music whenever we could. We swapped books, talked about our great loves (everything was big and great back then), and raised as much hell as young people could in those years.

Thanks to our parents' watchful care, we did not stray off the track. I would like to think that if some day, for some reason, I found myself lost at sea, Bland Ashiku – no matter where he is – will climb to the top of his imaginary tower and will sing a song and light a torch to guide me back to shore. He will lead me to the port. Here is what he said when we had our conversation:

If we're talking about over 30 years ago, at that time I was a teenager. The regime back then fully intended for all the citizens to be as equal as possible, from birth to death, with no differentiation between gender, age or wealth whatsoever. That's why the party had designed every element of life based on the principle of uniformity. Everything, from maternity homes to baby clothing, the planning of towns, the architecture of the buildings, housing, schools, work centres, school uniforms, work uniforms, entertainment and sport facilities, barber shops and hair styles, office and school furniture, types and amounts of food, relations between people, love, respect for parents, hate, divorce: every tiny little bit of life, the limbs, organs, and senses of what they called 'our new man' was programmed to be shaped by this uniform mould.

I guess it had taken far from common powers of imagination to design the uniformity mould down to the minutest detail, and turn it into a rather complex mechanism where the human dough was cast, then steadily stirred and blended together with generous doses of Marxist-Leninist spices and protective ideological preservatives, to produce an external impact, a resistant and obedient tool for the great class struggle. Furthermore, this mass was pushed down and duly processed in the pipelines where the education of this 'new man' took place, and then they came out on the other end like a string of sausages out of a meat processing equipment in a salami factory, supposedly ready for the new life.

I was meant to be one of those sausages, but things didn't work out exactly as the regime would have liked. I say this without boasting, and with indifference. It's true that the state operated with extreme commitment and responsibility, and achieved high results. Despite all of this, there were times when a tiny loophole made it possible to slip through the fingers of this fastidious control. I, for one, was an example of this, and this was due to the work done by my parents and my relatives, who from a very early age had kept warning us against ever talking to any one about what was discussed within the walls of our home:

'You mustn't tell a soul, not a living soul. Listen to Mom, I beg you, remember what Dad said, no talking to anyone, ever, we beg you!'

It was like they were hiding a thin needle in a secret fold under the lapel of our conscience. A very sharp, thin needle, invisible to strangers. It was with this needle that, when nobody was looking, we would prick the membrane of the sausage within which we had been packaged from the inside, and try to look at the world with our bare eyes. But until we reached a certain age, only the grown-ups were allowed to wear this imaginary needle, though I believe that we deserved to wear it much earlier.

Man tends to forget easily, but those were very difficult and rather painful times. I remember a story my Dad has told us many times, about a talk he once had with my younger sister, and how awfully sad the whole thing had made him. It all happened during one of my grandpa's visits. Dr Naim Vreto, a retired veterinarian, my mom's father, had come from the capital to visit us, and was spending a couple of weeks with us in the little town of Pogradec, where my father had been appointed director of the Amateur Comedy Theatre some years earlier. My dad was taking my sister Alba to the kindergarten, and on the way there he must have kept reminding her not to mention any of the stuff discussed with grandpa at home to her friends or the kindergarten teacher. At some point, my sister, who couldn't have been more than three or four years old at the time – way too young for the serious reaction that followed – had told him: 'C'mon, daddy, don't you worry, I know, sure I won't, or uncle policeman will put us in jail.'

***

I was born in Tirana in 1968, and did the first two years of the primary school there. Sometime in 1974, nearly two years after the fourth plenum of the Albanian Central Committee – which was a sort of an echo of the Chinese cultural revolution and supposedly dealt with art and culture issues in Albania – my dad was transferred to the small town of Pogradec, and appointed director of the amateur variety entertainment troupe of the town. Until then he had been an actor at the National Theatre, drama professor and head of the drama department at the Institute of Arts, but mainly he was very well-known because of the roles he had played in some rather popular movies of those times. He was so popular that people would greet him on the street, addressing him with the names of his characters. I used to wonder how many people my dad knew, though now I know that he had no idea who most of them were; these anonymous people, a thing which made me so proud in my childhood, and still does.

I guess that when I was a child, I wasn't able to define the reason for this pride, but that did not stop me from having a wonderful and very special childhood, mostly thanks to my mom's and dad's profession, and that of both my grandfathers – my mom was a paediatrician, and her father was a well-known veterinarian. My paternal grandfather was a famous pharmacist. Not many other children were so lucky as to get into the Albanian film studios 'Kinostudio' and the National Theatre as a child, and later on, a lot more often and more freely, into the Culture Palace of Pogradec. I remember watching the rows of spectators and the show from behind the stage curtains, the stage workers letting down and raising the curtain, the make-up artist powdering the sweaty faces of the actresses. Such nostalgic memories. I remember the secret pleasure coming from the knowledge that the 'bad guy' in the black leather jacket, stroking his huge moustache and brandishing that black German machine gun, was none other than Uncle Pëllumb, a friend of my father's, who after the show often came over for a drink at our place.

While most kids were terrorised by doctors, I went freely in and out the polyclinic where my mom worked, as if it were the Luna Park. The polyclinic, with the nurses all in white, and those beds covered in white cloth down to the floor, had become for me the best place in the world for playing hide-and-seek – though it never protected me from being scared to death of dentists.

My mom would take me to spend most weekends with her parents, and when I was old enough, my grandfather would take me along on his motorbike while doing his country rounds. Being one of the oldest veterinarians, my grandpa was one of the few people to own a motorbike back then, as all private vehicles were not allowed in Albania till the end of the eighties. Only the party VIPs, the high-ranking officials of the army, the administration, and factory and plant directors drove in cars in those days. A continuously shrinking number of mostly medical professionals were also allowed the privilege to use one, though whoever could find a bicycle and afford to buy it rode in one. Otherwise, it was public transport, which remained quite medieval-like up until the late eighties. Railway transport has today become nearly extinct. In the country, Grandfather Naim would check the sick animals, while I would play with the village kids, eat figs and jujube, or play with the cats.

Grandfather Aurelio rarely took me to his work, but he would take us for walks, and every day before siesta he would tell us cowboy-and-Indian stories, which I believe he invented on the spot. I tried to imitate him, when my sister was born, and a lot later, when my daughter was born, but I don't suppose I could ever get close to grandpa Aurelio's storytelling talent.

I finished elementary school in the small provincial town of Pogradec. After having lived there 11 years, the locals would still secretly and not without scorn call us 'the folks from Tirana,' whenever we returned, and when I was in Tirana, especially my first years at high school, I always felt I was some sort of an alien from the province. It was much like what the main character in Tasso Boulmeti's film *A Touch of Spice* would describe like this: 'In Istanbul they saw us as Greeks, and they sent us away as Greeks, whereas in Greece they received us as Turks, and saw us as Turks.'

A lot of other people had similar experiences. Whole families were often transferred from their hometowns and sent to other regions. It was a normal thing in those days, and though I always say that I personally really did have a beautiful childhood in that small distant town, for my parents those 11 years were without a doubt very difficult years. We were too young to understand what was really going on. However we had this feeling of our lives being left there, pending, as if in a sort of an infinite wait, in an endless attempt to return to Tirana. Pleads and refusals, promises, efforts and disappointments went on forever. My parents didn't know back then, that my father had been sent away from Tirana with marked as someone marked 'a person without the right to return' in his political records. Only after eleven years something happened: there seemed to be a slight softening of the regime and its ways, and the fatal remark was somewhat overlooked, and my dad was appointed director of the 'Alexander Moisiu' Theatre in Durres about an hour away from Tirana, where all our relatives lived.

My brother and I had been going to school in Tirana for several years before we moved to Durrës, but we had continued to spend the three months of the summer and the other school holidays in Pogradec with our parents. After having moved to Durrës, we spent at least two months by the Adriatic coast: sunbathing on the beach, fishing, real adventurous, free souls. I've often found myself thinking that Tom Sawyer and Huckleberry Finn did not do much more than we did. Maybe I'm exaggerating a bit, but I really can't say what else it would have taken to make us more unique and free.

I've always disliked the term 'refugee' since the time it started to be used to describe anyone who had left Albania and moved to another country. In my view the real refugees were the ones that climbed the walls of the embassies in July 1990 and arrived in overcrowded ships on the shores of Europe. No doubt this doesn't make me better than the ones that sneaked away, crossing the border or otherwise, because I also dreamed of doing the same, but I didn't have the courage. Instead I managed to leave with a regular passport and visa, and a load of romantic fantasies. I was certain that I would find a job. I had, after all, my documents with me, my diplomas and grade certificates, everything notarised.

Had I had a different nationality, and a regular permit of stay, with the papers I had with me I would have become an English language teacher, if not in Athens, then in some village private language school.

My idea was to find a job, rent a little apartment and once I had the financial means start going to an art school and study painting. However, all my dreams went up in flames. After a few months all my plans had turned to ashes. Nevertheless, those four to five years in Greece were a big window of experience for me. Greece back then was what Albania should have been like, and if Albania today were anything like Greece then, that would be a fabulous thing!

In Greece I was always on the look-out for work, and for all kinds of jobs. I worked wherever I could and I'm happy about this, because being young and adventurous helped me romanticise the many difficult moments I had in those days. It's not the same as when four guys who have a family to feed set out looking for work and a better life, and end up in an unknown island with no money to go back. There were four of us 24-year-old rolling-stones, and it was difficult, yet I recall with nostalgia and affection the terrible week that we spent in Chalkidiki, those chilly nights we spent, the four of us lying huddled on the damp floor of a tiny unfinished bathroom in a house under construction, the indescribable cold and the fear of being discovered by some watchman, but back then it was all just an adventure for us. A bitter adventure, perhaps, but still very much an adventure.

The worst thing about that period was being an illegal immigrant, which was eventually the reason why my wife and I left Greece. I'm convinced that we Albanians will only start respecting ourselves after we have freedom of movement, which we actually have got with the Schengen agreement now in place, and it is only then that others will respect us too.

Let us go back in time and understand what happened when we finished university. Let's remember that last meeting of the youth organisation, in which everyone of us had to give in and put our fate in the hands our school friends' vote and let them decide the future place of work for us. Nowadays there are loads of TV reality shows in which the group decides in which part of the world you are going, which dangerous river, where and how you cross it, where you spend the night, and what kind of wild beasts you meet on the road. Young boys and girls, suntanned and weathered by the sun, the rain, and the wind, try to survive in an unfriendly environment using whatever they can get their hands on. At the end of each episode the participants wait full of anxiety for the group's decision on who will remain, and who will leave. 'Expedition Robinson' and 'Survivor', if I'm not wrong, are such reality shows. Everything planned and rigged to test the poor individual. Didn't our last meeting resemble one of these reality TV shows, a sham drama, a farce, because it was clear to everyone that in the end it was not us who were going to decide?

As a result of this, the student friendships that we had built in four to eight years would be tested and even if you would not mind the final results of that meeting – again 'the ego', the personality, the achievements, the friendships until then unspoiled, were tested and often broken under the weight of disappointment. What would weigh more? In these meetings, you would notice some young party candidates, who even in the last breath of the regime, in 1990, again aimed at having a career, finding a comfortable place in the ranks of the party, because of their conviction that from there they would still show how capable, visionary and rich in perspective they were. The girls that had managed to marry before the end of university were in a favourable position, since they would remain in the towns, in Tirana, in Shkodër, Korçë, Vlorë and not go to the villages. This was an achievement. The carefree single girls, who had enjoyed their school days, were usually deported by a general vote to the villages. Certainly, the boys who did not have 'warm shoulders' had to try the country life too. Thought up by the party apparatchiks, this experiment aimed at breaking any kind of solidarity among students. At the end of the day, however, it was the students who, only after a few months, became the catalyst of the transformative processes in the country.

❦

I often think about those days. Every time that Lina, Maja and I set out for the south in the summer, actually everytime I pass by Gosa e Vogël village, it absolutely crosses my mind. And I can't help saying, or thinking: 'There it is, daddy's school!'

Did you know that at first I was appointed to work in some godforsaken hamlet, which even the State Secret Police had difficulty with? Luck had it that after my appointment, my dad ran into an acquaintance of his, a police investigator. On hearing where I had been sent to work as a teacher, the investigator chuckled amusedly and told him that my village was such a hole, which even the police hadn't been able to find a few years before that, after some murder had taken place. After this, dad pleaded with everyone he knew, 'begging for a pardon,' which I was given at some point, and was sent to another little hole some two hours away by bus. I'm glad that the miserable little village where I taught for a year or so has now grown into a little town with normal looking buildings, shops and everyday life.

I hope by now that the houses all have running water. I

remember chasing after my pupils who would cut class to go and stand in line at the water queue. There was this metal pipe in the centre of the village, a sort of a water tap, sticking its long rusty neck out of the mud, and near it a caravan of walking stones and buckets, jerry-cans, pitchers, jars, bottles, anything that could hold water. The queue came alive like a demented kite every time water started rushing – dripping is more like it – out of the rusty spigot of the old pipe, as my kids and the other folks rushed from all directions and grabbed their receptacles to claim their places in line. In these cases I tried to look and sound strict, and I might have given a couple of them a slap or two on the neck in some extreme cases, which is really ugly. But my strictness as a teacher and my feigned slaps was more like caressing when compared to the beating they would receive from their parents if they did not manage to fill up their water container and bring some water back home.

There were plenty of beautiful things and a lot of sadness in the life of a village teacher. However. when I think back, my situation was much better than that of my brother, who worked for many years as a math and physics teacher on a snow-topped mountain region somewhere in the highlands of Peshkopia. I was quite lucky that my village was only two hours away from Durrës, where the rest of my family lived at the time. I couldn't wait for the end of the week when I would rush off to Tirana, and of course pay-day! I proudly delivered my salary straight home at first, and kept only a small amount for myself. But not long after, I would be asking my parents for a hundred here, and a couple of hundreds there, and in the long term I was spending more of my parents' money than I was giving them. A couple of months after I had started to work they stopped taking my money.

❋

'Put your salary there,' and they pointed to a little wooden box made by the Artisan Factory 'Migjeni,' which we had on a table in the hall. 'It'll be there when you need it.' In this way I could see for myself when the money was running out, and wouldn't screw up completely. When I asked my dad about this recently, he couldn't recall any of it.

I wonder how we made ends meet on those meagre salaries back then? Albanians were paid every 15 days back then, as they are now too, I guess, and my parents, I recall, regularly borrowed a couple of hundreds from relatives or neighbours to make it through to the end of the fortnight.

It might sound trivial, but sheer routine and such trifles filled the palette of our life back then. I remember my breakfast, the one I took to work daily: a ten-centimetre sandwich made of two thick slices of dark bread (as organic as it can get), a tragically thin slice of feta cheese, and two or three home-pickled red peppers, boiled in vinegar, olive oil, garlic and bay leaves by my mom, everything wrapped tightly in a sheet of newspaper. The smell of it was strong and very inviting, I'll say.

There was this young teacher at the school, Moza, who later became the school's deputy principle. She was also the youth secretary, so she had an office of her own, and there was this strange appliance in her office, a thick brick with some sort of a labyrinth carved in for the coiled wire to go in and a cord, which was plugged into the electrical socket on the wall. They were used as a heating at home or elsewhere, but also for cooking. I think we called them 'resistance heaters'. To heat our breakfast we would put the thick slices of bread on top of the 'resistance heater' and toast it. I guess elsewhere they were called toasters, and it might have been slightly more modern, but ours did the job just as well, and kept the place warm too. The office was soon filled with the wonderful fragrance of toasted bread. Moza, who was fond of me, would prepare tea for the two of us. Though she was some years older, and important, I would often tease her nonstop.

Some school kid who had a cow at home would bring us a bottle of milk from time to time. Milk like everything else was extremely scarce back then, people lined up at the dairy shop from two o'clock in the morning every day. Freddy, the gym teacher, who often made fun of everyone, couldn't resist saying every single time: 'Your milk looks fine, my boy, it seems like it hasn't been tempered with cow piss today.' I still do not know if that was true, but the legend has it that cow urine was the only ingredient one could mix milk with to make it look thick and not watery. While the tempering couldn't be proved, the milk was very popular among us village teachers. From time to time, I would accept a bottle of raki from some kid who was desperate not to fail English, or Military training, which I taught, but I always paid for the milk, regardless of whether it was enriched or not with the urine of the cow. On those days I would return home feeling like a hero, proud of my contribution in the struggle for securing our daily food.

Moza was very pretty, had jet black hair and a straight, retroussé nose, but as much as we could determine, she did not have a husband, a fiancée, or a boyfriend. So I often said: 'Moza, since you made no tea today, why don't you put on a pot of Turkish coffee, and after enjoying the coffee together, we will turn your coffee cup upside-down, and see what life has in store for you. It's a long time since we read your coffee.' She knew I was no fortune teller and had no idea of coffee reading, but still she would swirl her cup slowly, then turn it upside-down and we'd wait. Sometimes I did the reading, but more often there was a woman from the village who came over and did most of the coffee reading, but her fortune readings never aligned with my foolish predictions.

My fortune telling would generally sound like this: 'You will meet a painter at the art gallery in the coming days, who will one day become very famous. Your portrait, the one he will paint very soon after your encounter, will be his masterpiece, and it must be locked in a safe with a thousand keys because there, you see this tiny square at the corner of the cup – that's the sign which means that one day your portrait will stay side by side with Mona Lisa's…'

'But there's no art gallery in Durres,' Moza would say blushing. 'Say, what if we could go to Tirana on Saturday, your auntie lives there on "Myslim Shyri" street, doesn't she? If by any chance you are late for the last train back, and the chances are that you are going to be late, because the mysterious painter out of the coffee cup will sweep you off your feet, you can always sleep at your auntie's.' I continued grinning.

Moza is one of those rare people, who I call the pillars of the state. People like these, be they state employees, military or ordinary citizens, maintained their dignity, and the dignity of their profession even in the most difficult situations when normal life gets off the rails, and when people were no longer citizens but simply human beings, and they reminded the others that they should do the same, and they did so even in the most tragicomic situations that our country was going through then. We're talking about the nineties, when we were often so near to being beaten to death for no reason by the so-called *Sampistë*, the special forces. They would have the line bus pull over, pull out and beat up and kick around every young man whose hair was a bit longer than the norm. One day they stopped the bus, and ordered me to step out without any reason, but Moza stepped up and beat the living daylights out of those goons. Her face flushing – because Moza would blush instantly, out of shyness, or in this case anger – she talked them down as if they were some fifth-grade school boys: 'This young man is a teacher at my school! You have the right to ask for his documents only. As long as he is on this bus, I, the principal of the school, am responsible for him.' Deputy principal, actually, but good for her, to have thought of that. Now her face was red hot mostly with shame for having passed for the principal. I was petrified, I had no documents on me, only a diary notebook, full of sketches and some nudes, and some notes, some of which would have landed me in big trouble because of their 'condemnable' character. And by the way, I still have that notebook today.

I think that during that year in the school village, I learned more about human relations than about my teaching profession. I too, with the rest – though I had nothing against teaching – felt that the sound of my teeth rattling with cold was louder than the sound of the chalk on the blackboard. If I close my eyes now and lie down, that year can really turn in my mind into a Miazaki sort of movie, and could be called, 'The flying school of Little Gosa.' It was really a year in the air, in the clouds. The state administration was hanging in the air. The parents were hanging in the air. The society was hanging in the air. We were more or less living almost as if we didn't know that the world is round, we followed our daily routine, went to work, got together, loved and hated, but we did all these things while constantly shifting towards an edge, with no idea of what was there for us once we rolled down that edge. All the people that I knew, as far I can remember, were in this state of being. One was trying to get a visa to Italy, another was waiting for a new 'exodus', and hoping that this time he'd muster the necessary courage to leave, another one was secretly buying dollars with his miserable savings to have them ready, just in case. No one was completely there, we were all halfway up in the air, as if we were experimenting with a flying machine, and there – there, at any moment, we might find the ignition key and take off...

And indeed, very soon after that school year finished I left for Greece; many others for other parts of the world.

It's been a while now since I have returned. Now I live most of the time in Albania, but often that feeling of hovering in space returns, even without having had a drop of alcohol.

When I first moved to Russia, I would now and then walk to the window and take a few snapshots of the Siberian landscape. I'd take pictures of our yard, which was covered in snow for most of the year – the tall straight pines, our neighbours stooped under their heavy coats, hats, and their shopping bags, dragging their winter boots along the trodden trails in the snow, the stray dogs running up and down so they won't freeze, the squirrels performing their seemingly meaningless acrobatics up and down the pine trees, and the crows and the pigeons fighting their endless food war by the garbage trolley – and send the pictures home to my sister to let her see where her brother lived. I knew that in the evening when she got back home from work, she would visit my parents and show them the photos.

I could imagine my parents' reaction: 'Oh dear, oh my poor, poor boy,' I can hear my mother sigh. I first went to Novosibirsk, the capital of Siberia, and the city of my wife Lina, in 1995. That first time, I barely managed to hold out for three weeks only, out of the two months permitted by the Russian visa. The biting frost and a strange feeling of having been deported made me take to my heels. I returned the next year, in September 1996, having decided to stay and live there, since we were expecting our first child. It took three days to fly to Siberia back then, I had to change three to four airlines, and I had to spend one night in either Belgrade, Sofia or Moscow. Communication with relatives and friends was very difficult then, it was mainly by fax, but that too was rare.

I recall, it must have been a few days after my grandfather had passed away, when I received a fax from my father. I had just come home from work, and I remember being so happy when Lina told me that there was a fax for me. I sat at the kitchen table, happy and excited, but my eyes caught the bad news immediately, and I started to cry. My grandfather was so very far away, farther than anyone can ever be. It was when I received that fax that it became clear to me how far away I really was from Albania.

I suppose all of this has now changed with Facebook, texting, Skype and mobile telephones. Although my parents are still quite resistant to the idea of social media. It is only one year ago that my father finally agreed to have a mobile phone, but he still hasn't got the hang of texting or skyping. They still prefer to communicate mainly by land line.

I'm certain that I'm rather smart, extremely smart, way too smart, but I'll have to accept that I'm also totally superficial, which makes it impossible for me not to feel 100% Albanian. Anyone who denies any of these characteristics is no real Albanian, no doubt about it.

I feel as Russian as my citizenship permits me, and as far as I can handle liquor. I was thinking today, that when I got here in the late nineties, the people were considerably confused. Everyone was busy doing their own thing, constantly on the lookout for some opportunity to make money, looking for an angle here and there, looking for a sales pitch, in no mood for chauvinism and patriotic games: the general and main objective was building a home and thriving. Now everything seems different. They travel, they tour the world.

There are some really good contemporary Russian authors, with a critical and analytical mind, not known in Albania as far as I know, such as Tatyana Tolstaya, a descendent of the great Tolstoy, if I'm not mistaken, a very sharp-minded lady who my father has read more than me, Victor Pelevin, Yevgeni Grishkovetz, Alexey Slapovsky, and a lot more. None of their works have been translated in Albanian. Even in this, we, Albanians, remain superficial. None of the greater works of Solzhenitsyn, let alone the contemporaries have yet been published in Albania. I have observed that there's been very little good cinema made in Russia in the recent years compared to its astounding achievements and contribution to world cinema in the past. There have been just a dozen of really good films in a couple of decades, though technically the Russians are very advanced. Good pop music is more or less non-existent. It might seem that, because film and music are conceived to be consumed instantly, not like literature which can wait locked in a drawer for many years, the composers feel obliged to turn to disgusting compromises, because they haven't got the time and the patience to conserve their work imprisoned in a plastic CD. In all the cases, whatever sees the light of publication or makes it to the screen or stage in Russia dodges politics, at least inner politics. What deals with politics must have gone to the drawer. So, in this respect I feel bad both as an Albanian and a Russian, because neither in Albania nor in Russia are there many good films made and good contemporary music composed. No doubt we, the Albanians are the champions of non-creativity in both fields.

As to why I chose to start a business in Mexican cuisine, I believe we are as much Mexican as the Mexicans are Albanian, when it comes to food. We Albanians cook and eat more or less the same things as Mexicans, the same ingredients, and with the same passion, except for the spiciness, I guess. Hot food is not really an Albanian thing. It is in Kosovo, though. There they love their chilli peppers. But in the long run, we Albanians differ from the rest of the world mainly because, though we live in the centre of Europe, we live almost in the middle ages, in terms of standards and parameters, but not in terms of the brands of beers and blue jeans that you see in Albania today. Many of them are fakes, though.

❖

I live exactly in the last country on the list of countries where I'd like to live. In the first place on this list, it's again my poor country, but with nonstop running water and electric power.

❖

I love travelling, but I hate borders. When I crossed the border for the first time in my life, I was travelling with a regular visa, but I was told to get off the bus, because the Greek military who stopped and checked the bus after we had actually passed the border control, supposed that my visa was false. I did convince their senior officer somehow that my visa was valid, but it seems I've developed border phobia. I believe I might have travelled with great pleasure to the West, if it weren't for the tedious procedure of getting a visa.

We have a fragile relationship with Europe. As long as we are threatened daily with the return of a visa regime, this will be a blow to the heart first thing every morning. Related to Europe, and being European, we Albanians really act as a body with two minds, with two personalities. As soon as we cross the border and are in a foreign country, we are transformed into other people, we no longer spit on the ground, or have a problem with not smoking in public areas, or beat the red light. In my view, we Albanians must really love science fiction, for all the cinematography, the music, the literature, the legal system, and a myriad of other elements which compose the world of the non-Albanians seem totally alien to us. In a way, they seem simply to be stage props.

We read books about France, while at home there's no water and no electricity, we go to an air-conditioned café to keep warm, and watch the news on the café TV screens, could well be the news from Mars.

One day, some years ago, as I was walking along the promenade 'Lazgush Poradeci', the one over the dam at the artificial lake in Tirana – did you know that it was called that? – I saw in front of me two gentlemen in beige raincoats, very similar to the ones which were so fashionable among the high officials of the Communist Party back in those days, that later became fashionable with the Democratic Party guys in the early nineties, to the point that people referred to them as 'the white raincoats.' One of the beige raincoats turned out to be none other than the former first secretary of the Communist Party, later the first president of Albania after the big changes, Ramiz Alia[4]. I didn't know the other guy. They were walking and talking at the same time. No one paid any attention, and I'm sure that no one recognised him, but for me, and since I had my camera, I took one or two snapshots, which I must still have somewhere.

I took the pictures probably driven by the instinct of the street photographer, or just because nowadays we can't help taking pictures of famous people. There, the man whose face wasn't that clear and recognizable in my photo. He has been one of the most important people in my life. A great injustice, that's true, because it should have been completely different, the most important people in my life should have been our parents, our teachers, our children, our buddies, our friends, our loved ones, and not him. But, alas, however strong the connection with my parents, my grandparents, my friends, and however great their influence was, they were destined to merely be the people closest to us, while the absolute right to be important belonged exclusively to Ramiz Alia and his cronies. Everything depended on them then. Nowadays, unfortunately, it's still the same. They were the ones who moved your family somewhere, they appointed your father director of the Amateur Comedy Theatre in the province, they chose which school you went to, they decided where you worked, and so on. The others – our parents and grandparents – were caring and full of affection, but not important, and the only thing they could do was to teach us how to bend to the will of these important people, so that we would not suffer the same fate of our grandfather, grandmother, or the aunt of the guy from the first floor.

It can make you laugh and cry at the same time, but even nowadays my dad – who is the person who has probably influenced my thinking and emotions more than anyone else in my life – when talking about people who've had problems all their lives due to their character, will say something like this: 'He can't keep his mouth shut, he talks way too much.' When I was young, I used to think that he said that to put me on guard, make me aware of what could happen if I talked too much, and the thing is that even now, when he speaks of someone who can't keep it shut, I'm convinced that he's in a way saying it for me to hear, because I tend to speak out all the time.

It is the only thing left to us, isn't it?

Lina and I were talking the other evening. 'Mom was asking,' she said: 'what does Bland think about the situation in Ukraine?' 'What do you expect him to say,' she had told her mom. 'Or do you have something to say?' she asked me. 'Of course,' I responded. 'How can I not have anything to say? I really think a lot about these things, because they can suddenly have an impact on our lives, for example, the visa regime might not be lifted for Russian citizens this summer.'

Furthermore, Albania is such a small country, and local VIPs are always somewhere in our midst, we run into them all the time. At least in Russia it easily seems like you are leading your own life undisturbed by these 'apparitions'. There is no chance that you would meet anyone important on the street, politicians or high officials. My wife doesn't know anyone from the IRS office, or the municipality, or social insurance. She pays her taxes, does her job, and that's it. In the afternoon she goes to the fitness centre, in the evening to a café and back to work the next day. On certain days she hands in the signed papers and money at the counter, and then bye-bye, gone she is to mind her own business. Instead, here in Albania, we can never get rid of the important people and the ones in their service. It was like this in the old days, it's like this now. You have just paid the electricity bill, when two nondescript guys turn up, each with a file under the arm. 'It's an inspection,' they will say, 'we need to check the electricity meter, tell us where it is?' 'Where it should be,' you respond. 'Look, you still owe 100 Lek, and you are risking a fine here, because you are late,' their tone is on its way to becoming menacing. 'It's not possible, we do not have any debts, we just paid, we are pay regularly.' 'Look here, we can always call for the task force...' What a bore! And it's like this every day.

Ok, let's get back to Novosibirsk. Just yesterday, my wife and I drove through the Kalinin square on our way home.

She saw me use my phone's camera. 'C'mon, why do you take pictures of this place, what for?' asked Lina, who is always telling me that I often take random pictures without a reason. She is right. I take a lot of photos these days. And then I forget about them. Like about the photographs of Ramiz, our former General Secretary.

'I photographed the Book,' I told her. 'The Book' is one of the buildings at the square, which reminds you of an open book, that's why they call it so. This square has not changed much since I first arrived in town in 1996. The same buildings, the same ugliness, though if compared to the 'Wilson' square in Tirana, it certainly stands out. I was in this square on the night when my daughter Maja was born. It was right after I had been to see her at the maternity home. I remember this every time I pass by. We stood there in the freezing cold, leaning against a kiosk in front of 'The Book' together with a student friend of mine, who had accompanied me to the hospital that first night. It was around minus 14 or 15 degrees, I remember looking at the temperature on the electronic clock of 'The Book,' and we drank 14% alcohol by 'Dr. Morgan' or something, celebrating Maja's birh.

That night should have been the most important event in my life. And when I think about it, it has been very important. Is anything else there that could make a man go out in the middle of the night, in the total darkness of our neighbourhood, at minus 20 degrees, in search of a ride in a city without taxis, and then get somehow to the only supermarket in the city, to buy diapers for your child? I could say the same about my coming to Russia, which absolutely changed my life. I had read about Russia and the Soviet Union all my life, but I had never imagined that one day, at the age of twenty-eight, I would come and live in Russia, work here, and become a Russian citizen, with a Russian passport, social security number and a health insurance.

These events should have been the most important ones! Or going to Greece when I was 23! That had also changed my life radically, because after 23 years of living in the same place, a small, socialist country, the most isolated place on earth, no one could imagine that the day would come to cross onto the other side of the border. Had we had multiple lives, these would have been the most important events, but as a character in yesterday's movie said, 'There's only one life for each of us, the same life all the time, it continues from our birth to our death, and that is why we can't be talking about a new life.' Hence, the most important event is not always the one that simply changes the course of events, but events which make people look life straight in the eye and say: this is me, and these are the people I live with.

On the other hand, one can say that the most important events that influenced my life actually took place without my participation, thousands of kilometres away. Here I refer to the changes that swept through Eastern Europe in the eighties, when our lives changed direction forever.

The more conscious one becomes of the arbitrariness of his or her destiny, the more painful it becomes. The capacity to take everything with a certain dose of humour and to make everything relative, saves you. Aren't all our efforts to become unique and free made with the purpose of escaping our 'destiny'? Do you really think that it's better to live intensively or to describe and to document that intensive life? The description and documentation are important, but there is something lifeless and rigid about it.

I guess I had more hobbies as a child. When I was young I was crazy about bird-hunting. I've been fond of art all my life. I used to draw and do a bit of painting. Later I tried to learn how to play the harmonica, and though I have no real ear for music, for quite some time I managed to play a few recognisable tunes. I've been very fond of literature and cinematography since I was a child, and I remember that when I was about 13, I started writing a novel in the spirit of *The Boys of Paul Street*, by Ferenc Molnar, and *A Captured General*, by Skënder Hasko. I gave up writing that book when I could not find the right words to describe certain events and moments. I guess I had no story to tell, that's why I got stalled on that doorstep for such a long while.

Later my strongest passion became drawing and painting. My social circle was saturated with friends and conversations that had something to do with art and painting, and many of my closest friends either painted or wrote, or read avidly in their free time, and some of them were even studying in the Artistic Lyceum or the Academy of Arts.

At home we were crazy about films. I also often went to the theatre, not only to see what my father staged, but also during the rehearsals which I was allowed to see. I was brought up in this spirit, so later, when teaching, I tried to organise my class like a little show, though without a stage and curtains.

These passionate hobbies have followed me more or less all my life, though I'm not doing any painting now, probably because of the camera. I started taking snapshots with a half automatic in Greece. Tourist's photos. Later on, in Russia, I bought a Zenith, not expensive, but a very good one, and since then I've had several digital cameras. I carry my Canon along wherever I go. I'm fond of street photography, capture different moments, different places, I love to photograph people, their portraits and their spontaneous movements. I don't really like my subjects to pose, probably because of what my grandpa Aurelio used to say: 'The best photos are the ones taken when no one is aware of the photographer.' I must have been a child when he first said this to me, but it has stayed with me, and so I tend to photograph people when they are not aware of me.

I still like to write, but as in the case of my first novel when I was 13, I've not been able to finish any of the books that I started, though they all start beautifully and I think they have important and interesting subjects. I start them, and then drop them, and I really feel sorry, because I really like the art of writing. Another dream I have is to make a movie, write the script and direct it. I have several scripts in my mind, one of them I'm going to complete, by all means.

Then, my biggest dream is the creation of an agro-touristic centre, a little village somewhere in the south of Albania, which I can take care of together with a group of close friends.

Almost every time that we are within our social circle, we have this dialogue:
- 'Where are we going?'
- 'With or without water, electricity and railways?'

People in America have an altogether different life. Our problems are unimaginable for them. The sheer energy of that place! Great energy and commitment. Everyone is so polite and always smiling at the airport, they must be well trained. Everything they do, they do it smiling, even when they are about to fool you, they fool you with a smile. Let's agree on this, work means work, working-out is real working-out, then in the evening a glass of wine. They do not lead our kind of life – all the day at work. And they do not have the kind of holidays we have!

Russia is very different from America. We resemble each other in many things, but ultimately there are rules in America. Work means work, salary means salary, vodka is vodka, order means order, fines are fines, stealing means stealing, police means police, tourism means tourism, and the government takes care of the rest, the complicated stuff.

Whereas here, along with everything else, there's also the burden of dealing with our government's complicated stuff. And however you look at it, in the long run it's us who get it up the ass.

Most probably we won't be here in 20 years, very few of us will have stayed. There is an end to patience, the same 'leaders' are coming and going, castling after castling, commissions are created anew to reform the justice system, to change the constitution, but they consist of the same old people, the veterans of the institutional and administrative chaos and disorder.

Naturally the questions that follow are: why this enthusiasm now about the changes in the system, when these changes are only cosmetic changes which are sold very dearly? Why are the people still so enthusiastic about the so-called new laws, that have been drafted by the same five or six experts, people who have made the same speeches and promises for the past three decades? Why didn't they make these changes 25 years ago, why not yesterday? Because, in reality, things remain the same.

So then, where are we going? My answer is nowhere. Most of the people with talent and education will leave the country gradually. It is only the corrupt crooks and those who can't go anywhere that will remain. It will be this way, if no radical and systemic changes are made to ensure implementation and continuation of the changes in the decades to come. All the other measures to strengthen law and order – for example threatening people with imprisonment to make them pay for electricity or water – will all fall apart once a new administration comes into power.

This happens because these changes are not systemic, but are carried out by pressing two or three buttons, which the future government will immediately set aside by expelling these officials from their jobs and employing new staff. If there are no fundamental systemic changes, all the improvements of the last years are going to be annulled in the first months of the new administration. The changes have to be legislative for their effect to be valid for many decades. The changes in the system require a parliamentarian majority, which seems to be so difficult to achieve. The present coalition government has a majority in parliament, and if they really wanted, they could take fundamental measures to strengthen the state. This goes beyond changes in the personnel or administration, beyond the coming and going of a loyal and dedicated police force.

That is why I think that it's only our entry into the European Union that would bring real change, because we are one of those countries, where the changes are always imposed from above.

And though there is this impression that the current government is very keen to have Albania join Europe, the truth is that we are really making very few changes, and we are asking Europe to change the rules of the game to suit our ambitions, to accept us in the club, and after that we will show them how good we are. Albania is more or less hoping for the same procedure, which made it possible to join NATO, but this time I don't think we will be successful.

Iris

> *Out beyond ideas of wrong doing and right doing there is a field.*
> *I will meet you there.*
> Rumi

I got to know Iris Luarasi through my work with the Albanian media after 1997, a most difficult time. What struck me in the wretchedness and the chaos of those days, was the fact that Iris and her friend Enno Alimerko, the founder of Radio Ime (meaning 'My Radio'), the very first private radio station in Tirana, radiated only optimism. Even nowadays, each time I meet my friends I get an overdose of goodwill and positivism.

Perhaps there are many things that I don't understand or feel or manage to share with my young new friend. Why 'young' and 'new', and who would I consider an 'old' friend? Would this mean that all the dear people I've met in the last two decades of being in The Netherlands do not equal my 'old' friends? Are my 'old' friends only the ones I can share everything of the past with, the ones who do not need an explanation about the pages of the communist dictatorship and the start of transition in Albania? No. Iris is only five years younger than me, but we have experienced the end of the dictatorship, the start of the transition and 1997 (the year when the Albanian state institutions imploded) in very different and personal ways. She experienced the last quarter of the past century as young people do, courageous and eager to survive at all costs. They fought in the name of life without doubting the meaning of their existence, as state structures crumbled and collapsed, as elementary norms were violated, as governing values were questioned and as the collective madness won the day temporarily.

My friends Iris and Enno never lost their way. They are my young friends, in spirit and in action. They are young due to a particular optimism and an incredible desire, amid all the chaos, the lack of infrastructure, and law and order. They worked hard to build their warm nest, to create a family, and to contribute to a better society.

Each time I visit Tirana, in addition to the joy of being back home, I am often weighed down by things that do not go well: stories of corruption, trafficking, falsification, bureaucracy, betrayal, murder, unpunished crime, and innocent people being killed daily. I am overcome by an undefined feeling of obligatory survival, I want and I need to meet my friends who are hospitable, accommodating, hard-working, and above all, who manage to function normally in an abnormal reality, which is almost absurd.

I often wonder how they manage to live and to enjoy their lives. Where do they find the strength, peace of mind and inspiration to create an oasis of normality in a troubled sea, in which the logic of political balance is often absent, in which the much-needed social solidarity of a post-dictatorship society is also absent, and where reflecting on the past is not encouraged? How important are the family, the borders, and the freedom of movement, religion and wealth? To what extent are their days, their present and future coloured by the general mood and trend? How much and how do they love Albania?

Iris and Enno have gathered at their house many kitchen utensils from all over the world. They are well travelled, and they both share a passion for cooking and good food. In that simple but beautifully furnished space, my friend Iris, a celebrated TV personality, well-known for her opinions on issues pertaining to Albanian society, is tamed and transformed into an attentive housewife and a devoted mother. The two of them, in their aprons and sleeves rolled up, would spend hours harmoniously creating the most delightful meals.

What you are going to read in the pages that follow is the result of a conversation with Iris at their dining room table, during a day off in between two of her travels abroad.

I was born and raised in communist Albania. Perhaps what I regret most is that I'm partially a product of that era dominated by the Marxist–Leninist teachings. A period that has inevitably left its indelible marks on me. Someone looking from the outside can't always recognise these traces of the past, but they are there. Those who scrutinise hard enough will no doubt detect the influence of the old system on us as a nation. I'm sure that all of my generation has in their subconscious something of those days lingering in them still. However, we were lucky to be young, so we have had the time to change and let go of the past. The older generation who spent most of their lives under the communist dictatorship are more affected by it. They have difficulties in adapting to the so-called 'transition', which is never-ending. Transition to where, I often ask? It resembles the waiting and weaving of Penelope, the Greek legend.

The start of the transition was painful especially for my parents. My father, who was in the military service, had to retire and give up his profession in 1992, even though he was still bursting with energy. Thereafter our family became solely dependent on the salary of my mother. It was a struggle for them to raise three children on a meagre income.

In 1991 I started studying languages and literature in the Faculty of Philology at Tirana University. I completed my first year with a grade of 10. I was fortunate that just at that time a new rule was established making it possible for all students who graduated with a 10 to receive a scholarship, which was more or less equal to a modest salary. This helped my family a bit. Thereafter my sister Keti started to work while still at high school, also contributing to the family income.

During my first year at the university, I started going to Radio Tirana. I began to assist the programming staff and I got paid for that. It was not a lot of money, but enough to buy new books that were until then forbidden from being published in Albania. So it was a period of buying a lot of books, by Freud, Dreiser, Hemingway, Stendhal and many other wonderful and well-known writers, whom we had never heard of in communist Albania. I had made a deal with a bookseller, who used to keep 'my' books apart until I was able to pay for them. Nowadays I see most of the young generation spending a lot of money on clothes. Certainly, I too like dressing up well, but when I was a student I really enjoyed possessing and reading books. I think in the past, people used to read much more than now, we used to exchange books, exchange thoughts on books, and everything else that was forbidden or taboo.

I started working when I was 18, so I've already been working for 25 years nonstop. In 1991 I worked together with Arjan Dodbida – who passed away and is no longer among us – on the programme 'The artistic literary magazine'. A few months later I was involved in the preparation of the morning programmes, which were the first directly broadcasted programmes of Radio Tirana. There I met Enno. In those years, Radio Tirana was the only station in Albania, and though I was very young, working with the morning programme made me feel very important.

Around 1993 or 1994 Enno and I thought of doing something special. We decided to focus on preparing a series of programmes about drugs, HIV, AIDS and sexual violence. All of these were taboo topics in Albanian society. A lot of Albanians did not know what AIDS was then. We started documenting various cases of violence and rape and we managed to interview one young man who was HIV positive. We also interviewed his doctor and I remember the programme was considered 'breathtaking'.

I think what made a difference was our ability to find a person who was willing to share his story. As you know, people's mentality has been to ignore and to deny by being silent about the disease. At that time in Albania there were only eleven registered cases, an unreliable number if you consider the immediate opening of the country and the unregulated flux of movement in and out of Albania. This was related to the lack of information in general. Our main interviewee, 'R', had a university education and was very open and willing to share everything that was happening to him. This was probably the best interview that we had done. After some time, he passed away. Two other men, also HIV positive, could not understand what was happening to them and were in denial. Their response to the disease was to immediately get engaged to be married!

I also recall the programme about sexual violence, for which we interviewed a girl that was raped and while visiting the prisons we came across one of her rapists, who came with a very different story. It was a kind of programme that got the interest of the public due to the intensity of the interviews and the thorough analysis of the issues, which were debated and looked at from every angle. For these programmes we were awarded a prize for the 'best radio programme of the year' by the Media Centre of the SOROS Foundation.

In those days' people did not yet own cars, which have now invaded our roads and pavements, so they stayed home and listened to the radio. Enno and I received the same award again in 1999.

During the tough days of the Kosovo crisis and war, I was directing a radio programme dedicated to the brothers from Kosovo who were forced to leave their land and flee to Albania, and their hosting families. It aimed at reaching Kosovo Albanians spread out in the region and in the world, who had lost touch with their relatives. I led a team of professional journalists and our work was observed by two BBC consultants and one consultant from the Public Radio of America. The programme consisted of 10 minutes of news and a 20 minutes' magazine. The title was 'In the name of humanism' and was broadcast by Radio Tirana, the first channel, and via satellite. Remember that in those days radio was an irreplaceable and indispensable medium of information and communication, whcih was massively listened to.

In 1995 I got sacked from Radio Tirana. We had just started preparing a morning news programme with the press review of the day. We had no budget at our disposal, but Enno and I nevertheless went and talked with all the editors of the newspapers, and asked if they would bring the papers free of charge. Lorenc Ligori, Edi Paloka, Armand Shullaku, Luan Rama and some other editors-in-chief of the newspapers agreed with our request. But many of these papers were very critical of the government and politicians of that time. Their views were in conflict with the Albanian Radio and Television (RTSh), which claimed to be public and to serve everybody, but in fact was a state institution totally at the service of the government. So, the opposition press review was not welcome.

I was called by the vice general director and told that I could continue with the programme only if I would not review two newspapers: *Koha Jonë* and *Zëri i Popullit*. Certainly I could not agree with that, and being a naïve young girl, just 23 years old, I tried to explain to the deputy director all the benefits and credits that RTSh would get if it served all the people and showed its independence. In the next programme, I remember that I read only the title of an article at *Koha Jonë* newspaper, which attacked the then President. That was enough for the programme to be qualified as 'weak' and for me to lose my job. This I experienced as the end of the world. I had just graduated with excellent results, and could not imagine, nor agree, that they would prevent me from doing what I really wanted – to work in radio. They treated me as an enemy. I was young and could hardly grasp the close relationship between my work and the politics of the time, even more so because I was not a sympathiser of any of the politicians.

Perhaps losing my job made me aware of the relationship between different actors in society, the duties and the responsibilities of the individual in relation to his or her work. I was full of resentment because at the only public station in Albania people were not allowed to think as free people, but had to keep in step as in the old days and flatter the politicians each time it was deemed necessary.

The politics of those days produced a blind militants' attitude, which I had to suffer from, though I had not experienced the old 'militantism'. During those days, I had become close to Rich McClear, the IREX director in Albania and consultant to Radio Tirana. I used to assist him with Radio Journalism and Media Management at the Journalism Department at Tirana University, where I still continue to teach these two subjects.

It was as a result of our experience at Radio Tirana that Enno brought the idea of creating Radio Ime, a project influenced and encouraged by Rich McClear. In 1995, McClear, together with Enno, had visited the first Albanian private television, TV Shijaku and the first private radios in Vlora and Fier. Influenced by this they began to look at the idea of starting a private radio station in Tirana. If it was possible to set up private stations in Fier and Vlora, then why not in Tirana? Enno planned everything and started putting the station together. At that time, I was working at the university and had given up hope of ever returning to Radio Tirana. Enno invited me to work together with him. I thought my dream was coming true: I would have the opportunity to work in radio again.

Radio Ime started in March 1997, during a very turbulent period in the history of Albania. Feverish days. I remember one day: we had just presented the news and gone to our 'usual' café near the office, when we saw for the gone time masked men all armed. We left and understood that the situation was getting really complicated. In the days that followed, the people – though few at the beginning – knew that a new radio had started broadcasting in Tirana, but they had no idea who was running it. The frequency of Radio Ime was 104.5, between the Voice of America and the BBC News. These were our first steps and there was a lot of interest.

Some months after Radio Ime started, I was offered a scholarship to follow a one-year internship at Boston's Public Radio in America. It was a wonderful experience. I met a group of competent people, good professionals who were modest, hard-working and had good dispositions. I would never forget them. I used to report for Radio Ime from Boston, for example when the great Albanian, Mother Theresa, passed away. After completing my internship, I decided to return to Albania. Staying in America was not an option for me.

I returned to Albania, in the first place, because of my relationship with Enno, secondly due to my passion for radio, and thirdly because I also enjoyed teaching at the journalism department of Tirana University.

No doubt Enno was and is my best friend. Although our story started as friendship, we are now connected by our love, our children, our families, and our profession. Had I stayed on in America I would probably have done some good there too, because I think wherever I would go I would still land with my feet on the ground, but I really had no plan. There is a difference between going there to study with a scholarship, and going there and starting everything from scratch. It is true that 1997 was a terrible year for Albania. I experienced living under curfew – and I will never forget it – as something painful, but also with a dose of humour. I recall on one occasion Enno and I were at the station until 1 minute before 20.00 hrs., the very last moment before the curfew. I also recall that my family 'invested' $1,000 in a pyramid firm when everybody was infected by this madness, just before they all collapsed. I think until 1997 Albanians believed in the state and in democracy. With the fall of the pyramid schemes and the state institutions, their illusions also collapsed.

The Albania of 2015 can't be compared with the Albania of 20 or 25 ago, in particular its capital city, Tirana. Certainly what makes a difference is the fact that we are no longer isolated. Especially here in Tirana one experiences rapid changes and the pace of life is felt intensely. There is a vast difference with smaller towns and cities of the countryside. The mentality of the people is also changing slowly. Many of the people who left and have lived abroad are returning to Albania, and some are investing in the country. There is a preference to want to live in the capital Tirana, which offers more possibilities, compared to other regions.

The return of the emigrants depends on the stability of the society and state, and the consolidation of the rule of law. The emigrants have often lived in countries where the rule of law prevails. They return with a mentality and ideas that promote development. I'm not prettifying the reality. There have been many occasions when I've asked myself: What are we still doing in this crazy country?

Now, as I speak with you, I realise that Enno and I will never consider leaving Albania to move abroad. It is not by chance that we have never applied for the Green Card. Even if Albania is not yet the country that we want it to be, I still think one can live here and with some imagination one can live very well. There are many special and beautiful places in Albania that you can visit and explore. On the other hand, you can choose your friends here, whereas if you are a migrant for many reasons you are often surrounded with 'occasional' friends, Albanian and autochthonous, because that is the choice you have.

It is not up to me to judge why the Albanian community in many other countries do not assert a strong influence in the countries in which they have chosen to live. It may be because they don't form a community, or because they are the product of an individualistic mentality, which might be changed only with time. In Albania we are near our own people, we have a certain standard of living and recognition. I'm a university teacher and lead an organisation that has a noble mission: it supports battered women. Here in Albania it's possible to make a good life for oneself from one's own sweat and toil, even if one is not involved in politics.

Of course, one of the fundamental reasons to remain in Albania is my family. It may sound primitive or patriarchal, but I like being near my family. The pressing times, the engagements, and the passing of time all play a role. I don't visit my aunts as often as I used to, but our relationship remains the same, and we continue to share a lot of affection and closeness. The same happens with my parents. They are in Tirana and I see them once in two weeks. This would be unimaginable 20 years ago. But now if I have some free time I choose to spend it with my children.

I feel 100% percent Albanian. I have very often met well-travelled people who react very well when I say I'm Albanian. Their travels have made them more open and free, more flexible and less prejudiced. But there are yet others who pull their faces and look away when I say I'm Albanian. For me this has to do with their own naivety and conservatism.

As much as I feel Albanian, I don't feel European. Most probably because I brace and admire the American way of life, and because I felt so accepted by Americans during my internship and my travels there. As an Albanian, I've never experienced being looked down upon or prejudiced in America. This is different from what we experience in Europe.

Rich McClear and his wife Suzy McClear, whom I talked about earlier, had a great influence not only on our profession, but also on the way we think about democracy and our understanding of the values of a free and democratic world. Our ideas of the functioning of a democracy, which is being installed with lots of difficulty today, has been moulded by the McClears, our mentors.

During the one year I spent in America I learned a lot and I tried to make the best of that way of living. I love America very much. When our first child, Noah, was born, I returned to work after only a few days as I could arrange to have him breastfed while working. I admire America's open-minded and practical ways. I don't know if people in Europe are so free, so fast, so practical, so solution-oriented. I really loved the rhythm of the American lifestyle. I try to live with that rhythm. And I want to teach my children the same values so that they grow up to be open-minded, and know how to behave in society and in public places, and not get stressed or discouraged by little hindrances.

I relate differently to the Balkans. Some years ago, Radio Ime was part of a South-eastern European network of radio and television. I was the member of the Executive Board and in 2005 I was elected the president of the network. For almost a decade we have worked and cooperated with colleagues from all over the region and particularly from the former Yugoslavia. At the end of the day, the personal exchanges matter and surpass all the stereotypes about 'the other'. I had to work with very good professionals from Serbia and Bosnia, developed friendships with them, and learned from them. I recall that my Bosnian colleagues were so tranquil and wise. It was then that I began to understand how important it is not to have borders. Everyone should have the possibility to travel to these counties, to communicate, to get to know the people. It was sad to see how far away we considered each other and how little we knew about them. The more I spent time with my former colleagues, the more I felt our commonalities, the things that connect us and not the differences that still keep us apart.

During the crisis and the war in Kosovo I also worked as a journalist in the field. What I understood – and this relates to my profession – is the importance of being human. Certainly I was moved by the suffering and the killings, and the fact that they were Albanians. They spoke my language, but above all they were people with their own lives and stories, with their own dignity, with their own losses and dreams. I tried to transmit this message during the programmes. And this makes me set apart the Serbs who are conscious and have accepted and realised what happened in Kosovo, and those Serbs who still do not see and accept what happened, and who still do not accept their loss. This world consists of open-minded people and narrow-minded people. The question is who will rule, who will take the power and take the decisions. I think that in general we as Albanians have to learn to be more proud of our country. We need to love our country more and not just save our patriotism only for football matches with our neighbours.

I'm convinced that everyone is particular in his or her own way, but some people have had the good luck of discovering this and pursuing their individuality, while others never discover and explore their particularity. I think I have the ability to call a spade a spade, to call things by their name, and that makes me free. Being this direct has not always helped me in my professional career, because most people do not value such direct communication. Living in a patriarchal society doesn't make that any easier.

Enno and I are Bektashians. We follow the Bektashi order, liberal Muslims who drink alcohol and eat pork. I believe in God, but I don't perform and practice any of the rituals. I look forward to all religious feasts and celebrations, including Christmas. We start preparing and buying presents for Christmas months in advance, certainly in accordance with our financial possibilities. Noah is a baptised Christian, following the wish of his godmother – Enno's sister. I think it's not a good idea to be brought up without faith and not knowing anything about religion.

I'm still involved in several projects. I'm less involved with radio ever since I've become involved with the issue of gender violence. Violence against women remains a big problem in Albanian society. The number of crimes in the family has increased and that is why I'm more and more focused on this problem. I lead 'the National Counselling Line', one of the first organisations set up in Albania in support of abused and violated women.

Some time ago I had an idea which now has become reality – to open a counselling office for the abusers. Some of them reach us through the justice system, but there are many violent men who have approached us for advice themselves. They have recognised that there is a need to change. They want to help themselves, which is a huge step in resolving this problem. From 1996 until now the centre has been serving and counselling thousands of women. Today I felt happy that my candidacy was approved and I'm part of a group of independent experts launched by the Council of Europe. This initiative aims to monitor the work done in member countries against violence and family violence. We are not creating a revolution, but we are on the right path and I'm certain we will change something for the better in our societies through these projects. What we do now counts for the present and for the future.

My dreams about the future relate to my children. I would not encourage them to become journalists like both their parents. I would prefer them following another profession. A good journalist is in constant struggle with the people in power, and though one might be right and tell the truth, it takes a lot of nerves and energy to be successful in our profession. Becoming medical doctors would be a good choice, because their life will be simpler and they will really be able to save people's lives.

My dreams about the future of the country again relate to the future of the children, the new generation. Albania should be different and better. An important and unstoppable process is getting near and reaching the standards of other countries, and joining the European Union without trauma, regressions and great hurdles. I believe investing in education would speed up this process. I think politics should not play such an important role, I would not want politics to play any role in my family life.

In one way or another we are all involved politically, from the one who gathers empty cans to the one who has been elected and whose duty it is to lead the country. With this sort of 'politics', your work, your income, the quality of life are related and dependent. I hope and wish that in 20 years' time, politics would weigh less in the life of Albanian citizens. In my view this would mean that the wise and the honest people can be in charge, can lead, and not the ones who steal through the positions of power they hold, the signatures they put for tenders, mocking and laughing at the average, simple citizen who doesn't steal. I would never want my children to see and accept this way of life as normality.

Lazri

Finding myself, I found company.
Cesare Pavese: 'Ancestors'

I meet Lazër Stani in my dreams. Sometimes I meet him in my house in Tirana, where we drink tea at the kitchen table, translating together a poem by Akhmatova. Sometimes we meet in a cafe and talk about a story without a title, inviting it into the light so that we can baptise it right then and there. Sometimes we meet and walk along the coast, sometimes we take a mountain path that winds through the forest to his birthplace in Pult. More often than not we meet at the Library of the Academy of Sciences in Tirana. Sunlight falls upon the covers of old and new books in this classical library which has become a dream library. The books watch us for the hundredth time. Smiling, they murmur amongst themselves:
  -'I told you they would come again, didn't I?'
  -'Yes, but a long time has passed and I thought they would meet somewhere else.'
  -'They recognise our power. That's why.'
  -'Speak for yourself. You fascinate them, mesmerise them. When they turned my pages they would often become sad, seemingly unwilling to go back among the people.'
  -'Well here they are, back again, for us. This is more important.'
  In the dream library Lazër and I turn into children who want to learn to fly at all costs. We read and read and talk passionately about everything we come across, perusing again and again beloved books, each time discovering new things while feeling utterly at home in that labyrinth of human knowledge. Our friends, persuaded by our commitment, share with us all their secrets, one by one. At the end of our encounter they give us wings and bless us on our way, out into the big wide world.
  There we meet another child, Luljeta, who in my dream already knows how to fly. She is my dearest childhood friend and Lazër's

life companion. Flying, she drizzles verses on the wings of birds, filling our sky with words that fall like stars.

I wake up. I call Lazër and we agree to meet in a real café – Café Piccadilly, near the Writers' League in Tirana. The city has been washed clean by the afternoon rain. The trees and flowers in the courtyard of the café threaten to engulf us with their lush exuberance. We try to talk about 'important' things, but we can't. Nature wants only worshippers. We agree to meet on the web.

Perhaps without realizing it, Lazër, we have grown up and are now getting old. We have become parents and life companions, property owners, public officials, councillors and chairpersons. Are these roles you dreamt about filling when we were young?

The laws of life and ruthless time work on us; they change us every single day. A person can't really know when he or she first began to dream. We can't know if we invented the dream or were born with it written in our genes. Slowly, from our first moment of awareness, we follow it, struggling ceaselessly to realise it. But the dream remains always distant, unattainable, though it seems close enough to touch. It is like a game of sky where you see the mountain breaching the horizon. You say to yourself – as soon as I get to the top of the ridge I will touch the sky, but when you reach the top you realise the sky has fled to the next crest. I wrote once that a man can't relinquish his dreams; neither in literature, nor in real life. There is always a gap between our dreams and our lives. We live at a lower level than our dreams and it's this that makes us persevere, trying to manifest them as long as we draw breath. We do not lose hope.

I only know that my childhood dreams have always been distant. They did not end with the slope of the hill in front of my house, or with the mountain across the valley, they did not linger under the umbrella of the sky settling on the crown of mountains that surrounded my birthplace. Once, I climbed with a friend up to the highest peak, gazing from there at the wide horizon, down to Shkodra Lake and beyond to the Adriatic. I was possessed by a feeling of grandiosity, a surge of spiritual triumph. It seems I had always suffered the pressure of a narrow horizon.

I loved maps as a school boy. It was by means of maps that I travelled all over the globe, from the Arctic to the South Pole. I imagined walking every inch of the cities, the villages, the mountains and plains of our planet. And when the world seemed small, I turned my gaze to the sky, to the distant stars. I understood then that solitude is the universal law of the cosmos; the nearest star is thousands of light years away and the stars too are condemned to eternal solitude. I didn't understand why the Creator had condemned us to loneliness. Years later I became convinced that loneliness is not only the law of the universe, but also a law within us, written in our genes. We try to liberate ourselves from it by every means available without ever really succeeding. I believe it's from here that literature, among other things, stems.

In the ongoing struggle, which simply translates as years lived, I have achieved many things. I have studied and I've learned, I have made a home for myself and my family, I have been married, raised children, I have experienced loss and have seen many beloved people depart, I have written books and left some evidence of my existence. But as I've already observed, the dream always recedes, like the horizon. It always retreats to the next crest and this provides me with an incentive to go on living.

❖

I have often thought about this: what makes me free. I've arrived at various conclusions to this question down the years, but I've always been convinced that a man or woman is born with his or her own freedom intact. I don't mean the consciousness of being free or the courage to defend it when it's threatened. We were brought up in hard times for freedom, living as we did under one of the harshest dictatorships ever conceived. And yet, I think I've been a free man. I have written a story, 'The idiot travels to America', which explores this issue.

I resisted the biggest threats to my freedom by nourishing in myself the idea of escape. When I stood in front of maps, I didn't understand why I could not travel to another place just because it belonged to another state and other people lived there. Our planet belongs to the people who live on it, not to governments or dictators who raise fences and build impenetrable walls. I used to think about running away at a very early age, although I never did run away. It was a secret that excited me and allowed me to explore endless possibilities in my imagination. It also made me somehow detached from reality so that I didn't pay close attention to my career or the place where I actually lived. I lived with myself and for myself.

I remember the anxiety and the temptation of one October day, when I was sitting on the bank of the river Buna[5]. On the other side there was an old church which seemed deserted. On our side of the river the churches had all been razed to the ground. All I needed to do was swim a hundred meters and I would be on the other side of the border, in another world, mysterious and unknown. A little further up the bank three soldiers were basking in the sun, guarding the border, relaxed, smiling and playful. It was painful to imagine them becoming ruthless killers, had I dared to jump into the water in an attempt to reach the far bank, the foreign side. It was a cold day and the ground on either side of the river was frozen. I was warmed by the idea that one day I would cross that border, dead or alive. So I went back to my voluntary – that is, compulsory – labour of corn husking, but the excitement had captured my soul, like the excitement of a first love.

Later I shared this secret with my friend Ndoc Deda (Shtëpia). For many years we spent hours, nights on end, discussing the idea of escape, making plans, convinced there was no alternative. What prevented us leaving was my grandfather. Soon after we graduated he got sick. I promised Ndoc that I would run away with him when my grandfather passed away, the first autumn after his death. I loved my grandfather and I felt I could not abandon him. My grandfather died and one year later my friend ran away, but I stayed behind in Albania. I was never to go. Our borders fell and in one way or another political freedoms were recognised. Running away did not make sense any longer. But the freedom 'instinct', as I like to call it, doesn't function only in one direction. There are many unfree people living in free societies. I think I'm a free person who pays the price continuously for my freedom. The cost of freedom is heavy in every epoch and in every society, but it's only the feeling of freedom that makes life bearable.

❋

I feel thoroughly Albanian. I don't have and couldn't have another identity, even if I wanted to. I come from an old Christian Albanian family. Generation after generation we have been Albanian, since time immemorial. I write in Albanian, I speak Albanian, I was born and brought up in Albania, what else could I be? Of course, being Albanian is not a choice: I was born in Albania and therefore my identity card asserts I'm 'Albanian'. Does it mean something? Certainly those eight letters mean something. A foreigner reading my passport tries to understand what it means, he uses his geographical and historical knowledge as well as information from newspapers, but this superficial significance doesn't concern me.

A man is more than a geographical notion. His is a personal history, particular to him and incomparable with the stories of others, unrepeatable. In using comparisons and analogies we often arrive at mediocre conclusions, if not entirely mistaken ones. For me the significance of being Albanian is something quite different: it's my history and the history of my family, the words that I uttered first, my forefathers resting in their graves, it's the culture, the history, the myths, the legends, the dreams, the whole life project. I love Albania and I live where I want to live.

Geographical labels don't mean much. I'm Albanian and European at the same time. Perhaps other Europeans make a distinction between the two, but I don't. European civilisation is rooted in the Mediterranean, the Greco-Roman civilisation and the values of Christianity. As an Albanian, I come from a nation that merged these two civilisations. A nation, a people, giving and taking not only emperors, popes and distinguished military commanders, but also words of initiation, culture, myths, legends and history. The Middle Ages brought real drama to Albanians, changing the national archetype simultaneously with the European one. At the same time, I'm aware that it's not only birthplace that makes one European. It is culture and a system of recognised values.

❖

If judged by my literary preferences I don't have a nationality, or rather, my nationality is human. On my desk there are always two books: the poetry of Borges, *The Gold of the Tigers* and his *Poems of the Night*. Books with poems by Yehuda Amichai, Cesare Pavese, Salvatore Quasimodo, C.P. Cavafy, short stories by Isaac Bashevis Singer, Amoz Oz, Julio Cortázar, Roberto Bolaño, Franz Kafka and many others make up my dear library, which has only one identity – the culture of mankind. And I certainly feel part of that culture, more than any other.

❖

It is difficult to talk about oneself. Now and then we received guests at our home when I was a child and I remember one of them once said to my grandfather 'You are a brave man!' My grandfather responded immediately with 'Lord, do not test me!' If by being a man one understands being master of one's destiny, I think I've always been my own master, both in good and bad times, especially when facing difficulties, when there was no-one at my side, when I became a stranger to the world, even to the people I loved. Kafka wrote in *Metamorphosis* about the drama of the individual, and Pavese has some beautiful lines in his poem *Ancestors*:

> *Siamo pieni di vizi, di ticchi e di orrori*
> *- noi, gli uomini, i padri - qualcuno si è ucciso,*
> *ma una sola vergogna non chi ha mai toccato,*
> *non saremo mai donne, mai schiavi a nessuno*[6].

As for being a highlander, it's a term which refers to a native or inhabitant of the Highlands. In Albania highlanders have a special quality, they are less genetically diluted by the incursions of invaders and culturally they have kept alive the ancient archetype, due to their centuries of isolation. But you can't judge people on their birthplace. I had an amazing childhood in the house where I was born, where life and death were in a fragile balance. It was a life full of stories – never-ending narratives, myths and legends. They made life beautiful, full of mystery and hope. However, I instinctively knew that as soon as I was old enough and master of myself, I would leave the Highlands. And that is what happened. I think I took much that was good from there, but not its vices. In my writings my birthplace takes a lot of space. I always return to it, as if to an impossible paradise, one which we lost with the sin of Eve and Adam.

Finally, I believe I'm emancipated, as I'm a free man.

I'm a good father and strongly bound to my children. I'm not only their parent but a friend, an interlocutor. One day my daughter Lea told me: 'You are my dearest person on earth'. Lea doesn't usually express her feelings and I often joke with her that she is made for politics and diplomacy. She is not like her older sister Lodia, who expresses herself more emotionally. This makes me think that I'm a good father, although I wish I could do more for my children.

You should ask my wife, and your friend, about the experience of being married to a poet. In the classical sense of the word, I don't think I'm a good husband. Life is hard and spouses fight for territory. In a 'successful' marriage individualities dissolve, a couple becomes one composition, as happens with composite chemical substances which then gain new qualities. My spouse and I have kept our individuality, we have not amalgamated, but we have still managed to stay together all these years.

I write, but I don't know if I'm a writer. If I write some good pages or one really good book in my life, I would be happy. I don't consider myself a martyr to literature. It doesn't make sense to me to live only for literature, although literature gives meaning to my life and makes it possible.

I don't believe in any grand ideology. Ideologies have brought a lot of misfortune to humanity. Take the communist ideology and its catastrophic consequences throughout the world during the past century. An ideology that is propagated in a very seductive way is a powerful instrument in the hands of criminal minds, otherwise called dictators.

An intellectual mind is not prone to belief, it's prone to doubt. I believe in the power of love. Something I don't love, I can't do.

※

People need to believe in something. Faith is peaceful, a comforting solution, which relieves us of our stifling doubts, our unanswered questions. As a child, one is very curious and inquisitive. I was so as well. While growing up and becoming mature, a man looks for answers to his questions, ready-made answers in science, in religion, in philosophy. The opposite happened to me. The years have not brought answers, but questions. Now I have more questions and fewer answers than before.

I believe humanity is still in its infancy when it comes to knowledge. Despite the progress of science and technology, despite the development of culture and philosophical thought, we still lack convincing answers to the fundamental questions: where do we come from, who are we and where are we going? The mystery in the world is colossal, compared with the few things we know, and I'm convinced that after a thousand or ten thousand years, if humanity still exists, our limited knowledge will make us look ridiculous. Do I believe? I know that I don't believe in most of the explanations that we have been given; I know that beyond our knowledge there is mystery, there is the unknown. What is this mysterious unknown that has power over our lives? Is there a universal project, and are we humans part of this project, designed by someone in the same way as we design computer games? Or is there another explanation – something more essential, something more elusive and inaccessible? There is no single answer. Even bio-centrism, the most recent and provocative theory put forward by Robert Lanza, doesn't provide an exhaustive answer, but he arouses interest and challenges us not to dwell in the shallow waters of our knowledge. I believe that there is something beyond coincidence and chance. Let us call this power divine, as people have historically identified it.

I initially started learning Russian by chance, when I was in my first year of high school. When I finished high school I could read the language and enjoyed it. The language itself did not have any influence, but it was through reading Russian that I managed to read the major works of world literature, which in those days could not be found in Albanian. In particular, I was able to read much forbidden modern literature in translation. Throughout my twenties, I had access to world culture only through the Russian language. These were important years for me.

The most important people in my life are my family. In my childhood, there was my grandfather, my mother, my father, my youngest sister. My grandfather was an extraordinary man. I was brought up with much love and care – in one sense my family pinned their hopes on me. They loved me so much and hoped so much for me that my fear of disappointing them is the biggest fear I've ever experienced. Once I disappointed my mother. I've never felt so bad in my life. She did not say a word, but I read her deep disappointment in her eyes, the sorrow in her face. It had to do with my exam results in 6th grade which were all average. I took an oath to never disappoint her again and from that time on my school results were outstanding. Even today my biggest concern is exactly this: not to disappoint the people I love, the people who have faith in me. It is not easy. The most important thing in my life today is still my family.

At the same time there have been important people who influenced my development. First of all my teachers Xhabir Topalli and Moisi Mozali, my professors Zyhri Bajrami and Bajazit Shehu. Prof. Bajazit didn't teach me. When we met he had retired, but we used to meet and take coffee together. Talking with him was very inspiring; he was always supportive and gave me good advice, although I didn't follow in his footsteps down the road of science. One of his pieces of advice concerned the English language. He insisted that

I learn English and used to say: 'I don't know English very well, but if it were possible I would happily transfer all my knowledge to your brain'. I've not met a man of such noble calibre since.

I don't really know how I discovered art and literature, but I think it's an affinity, a spontaneous sensitivity you are born with. It seems simply to be inside one, like the passion for reading, hearing and telling stories, gazing in solitude at the stars in the sky, listening to the river that flows nervously in its bed, walking alone in the forests as the sun is setting on the hills. The Alps, where I spent my childhood and adolescence, are the most beautiful place on earth, a divine masterpiece of nature. I think it's there from which my passion for beauty, for nature, stems. Then came the reading, the endless reading, of every book I could lay my hands on. When I was a student I wrote for the newspaper and then started writing fiction. My relationship with literature became so essential to me that I can't live without it. Once I dreamt I was reading some amazing stories that I had written myself. I hope I will be able to write these stories at some stage.

Nothing of which I wished to do, am I doing now. I would have liked to be able to maintain myself and engage only with literature. This is a possibility I don't have and I will never have.

I can say I've had two difficult moments in life. The first, when my application was not accepted by the university. I was rejected two years in a row even though I was among the best high school pupils of Shkodra district. I had made up my mind that if they rejected me a third time I would attempt to run away. If I didn't manage to leave, I would be killed. I could not see myself earning my daily bread with a spade and a pickaxe.

The second difficult moment happened when a story was spread about me running away and getting killed at the border. It was October 1990. When I was fired from my job that September, they expected me to run away, but I didn't fall into that trap. In angry revenge they spread a rumour which had me killed at the border as 'an enemy of the people'.

I've also had bitter moments when I've been disappointed by people I trusted and loved with all my heart.

And I had a lot of happy moments. Perhaps the most beautiful one was when my first story was published by *Zëri i Rinisë* (Youth's Voice) newspaper. The feelings of that day can't be matched. But I really have had many happy moments.

I don't look back. Let bygones be bygones. Whether beautiful or sad, the past remains the past and you can't live life over again.

The system was a mistake, a historical accident which was barbaric, primitive, criminal. Luckily it collapsed but we are still suffering the consequences. I always felt disconnected, as if I had nothing to do with it. That was my way of surviving that period.

❧

During the last few years I've been busy with documenting the past in the Museum of Memory. We remember so that we can live in freedom! This has been a fundamental priority when curating the Museum of Memory because unfortunately, dictatorships and dictators are not a unique phenomenon in society. They have repeated themselves since antiquity right up to modern times, causing untold murders, terror, suffering, as well as the usurpation and violation of fundamental freedoms and human rights.

We Albanians have a bitter experience of this. We suffered under one of the cruellest dictatorships, one which not only planted death and poverty, filling the country with prisons and concentration camps, but which turned the entire country into a prison. We are trying to capture and show this dimension at the Museum of Memory, mainly targeting the younger generation who are very uninformed or have access only to propaganda about our dark past. It is one thing to say that communism was bad, that our communist leader was a dictator, that innocent people were killed, imprisoned, locked up in camps so that the country ended up in misery, and it's something else to provide people with the facts about the crimes of communism and the misery of Albanians through documents, photographs – evidence that can be touched, seen, felt. Certainly, our project is only one small step, but perhaps effective as part of our effort as a society to detach ourselves once and for all from our past and the logic of the totalitarian mentality.

It is up to the Albanian people to build their own future. If we don't change, Albania will not change either. The Albanian people have to gain a vision of the future which is now completely absent. The Albanian have to understand that the world doesn't end at his or her garden fence and life doesn't consist only of today and the day after. Finally, the Albanian has to learn to think with his head and not with his guts, to feel with his soul and not with his stomach. I must say that I don't believe I will see Albania become the country I've always dreamed about.

What I'd like to share with the readers of this book? One of my short stories, 'Baggage delay'. Our history is unfortunately a history of delays.

Ladi

Festina lente
Latin adage and oxymoron meaning 'make haste slowly'.

Some people know how to survive, thanks to their capacity to resist. Some manage to survive, thanks to their capacity not to attract unnecessary attention and an ability to make themselves inconspicuous. They blend in with the environment in daylight, and even in front of television cameras they are able to remain themselves. In my opinion, one of the people who could best do this, under the dictatorship as well as in the transition years, is Vladimir Grillo (Ladi), the well-known Albanian sport commentator.

In those days, many of us who did not have the possibility to speak freely, to move freely and to get to know the world freely, lost a piece of ourselves with every passing day. It was a piece of dignity, a bite of freedom, a dying nerve, a thread of thought, a burning emotion that we had to hide deep and not allow to raise its head. The communist regime had conquered the land, the sky and the sea. The sky had become unreachable, and we, with broken wings, could only dream about it. The boats were stripped of their masts and oars so that they would not sail towards freedom. Movement from town to town, from village to village, or from alley to alley was controlled by an army apparatus of so-called 'friends', comrades, relatives, commanders, collaborators, well-doers, benefactors and other mobilised forces with one single purpose: to break the individual and the desire to be free. Almost everything that could potentially lead to freedom or any expression of individuality was controlled, manipulated and directed.

It would be interesting to look at the role sport had played under these conditions? How did sport allow an opening for an oppressed people to unfold their individuality? What was the significance of the only television station in the country that started broadcasting in the late sixties, if it could not reach and win the hearts and *minds of the masses and educate 'the new man' as programmed by the ruling party? How would this goal to create 'the new man' make use of this medium of mass communication?*

Here I would like to refer to Italo Calvino's reflection in If on a Winter's Night a Traveller: *'To be sure, repression must also allow an occasional breathing space, must close an eye every now and then, alternate indulgence with abuse, with a certain unpredictability in its caprices; otherwise, if nothing more remains to be repressed, the whole system rusts and wears down. Let's be frank: every regime, even the most authoritarian, survives in a situation of unstable equilibrium, whereby it needs to justify constantly the existence of its repressive apparatus, therefore of something to repress.'*

During the 1970s and the many years that follow, every Albanian (so not only the sport lovers) who could listen to the radio or watch TV during the week or the reduced-to-Sunday weekend has had the chance to see and to listen to Ladi's broadcasts.

Ladi, the oldest son of Zoica and Dhimitër Grillo, both well-read and well-known among their friends and colleagues for their approach of moderation and discipline, had studied languages and literature. After his studies he was appointed to the Cultural Department of the only television station in the country, Albanian Radio Television (RTSh). He started working for the programme 'Our common friend', promoting new publications, as well as broadcasting relevant artistic news and activities taking place in the country. The theme of the programme was slowly expanded to include discussions and reviews of books:

According to Ladi, 'the first book to be discussed was the poetry collection Iron Rhythms written by Fatos Arapi. Mevlan Shanaj, the film director was invited to the studio to participate in the discussion. The show was appreciated for its content, but not for its form, as students had also been invited. It had caused a stir as some of the girls wore short skirts, which was in contradiction with the directives from above and the spirit of the time. This was considered to be 'an exhibition of foreign ways of behaviour'. The programme was criticised for this, but was allowed to continue broadcasting. They went on to produce other programmes such as the 'The Epopee of the National Front' with caricatures of Bardhyl Fico. The cultural programme was aired three times a week.'

When the idea of creating a sports programme was launched, Ladi immediately revealed an interest and willingness to work on the new programme. He saw it as a new challenge. He saw the sports programme as an opportunity to reach a broader audience. He was also aware that sport did not leave room for theoretical speculations and political propaganda. Ladi's choice for television was not well received by his family. He was expected to continue in the tradition of his father who was an historian and his uncle, Odhise Grillo, who was a writer. In the end, his family did come to terms with his choice.

Ladi describes how emotional he was during his very first TV broadcast. It was a totally new experience for him, and he made some mistakes, but colleagues helped him along giving him advice and after a while he got used to the cameras.

Ladi was not alone at the RTSh. Skifter Këlliçi was already in radio and they were both inspired by the father of sport journalism, Anton Mazreku. Ladi made a modest and timid start, first in radio and then on television. Later when Këlliçi focused on culture, Ladi concentrated on the sport programme, which soon became a favourite programme for the few television viewers of those years. The television sets were sold 'with state authorisation' which directly derived from one's loyalty to the regime and one's position. At first he prepared the news and later also the sports magazine. A good tradition was established by adding commentary and inviting guests to the studio. Due to the involvement of known directors and actors, the sports programme was enriched and became very popular.

Ladi explains that 'A good journalist should know how to make sport attractive for all.' The sports' unit was expanded. Ahmet

Shqarri started the programme 'From one match to the other'. It might sound funny, but in those days people waited at the old post offices so that they would be the first to know the final scores of the matches in the other towns. Ahmet managed to get connected with all the districts of the country and get the results. Another development was the start of another programme 'Sport Education' that aimed at making sports popular, so that the people were strong and healthy in defending the fatherland. Everything in the programme was aimed to achieve this goal. Some time later 'Sport Reportage' followed. Attention was also drawn to traditional sports and games, as part of the artistic sports culture. Every year the Albanian television broadcasted all the bicycle tours in the country. Handball games were reported on and broadcasted too. The matches were watched with incredible enthusiasm at huge sport palaces in several towns, which could host up to 3,000 spectators.

Ladi relates how he was once summoned by the director of RTSh, after a live broadcast from the Sports Palace in Tirana. He was criticised for being too emotional and stimulating the uncontrollable joy of the sport lovers present in the Palace. He was told that this kind of emotion and joy were to be saved and shown only in the hall of congresses, in front of tribunes, and not in an activity such as basketball! From then on Ladi had to show more tranquillity and control during his broadcasts. He had to make an effort not to mix sport with politics, which is the aim of every dictatorship. Ladi goes on: 'It was difficult to find a pattern and balance in the reactions of the RTSh directors and the high party officials towards the sports broadcasts.'

During the popular years of 'The Sportive Rubrique', one of the functionaries commented that, 'the programme was good enough to compete with 'Dynasty', the film serial broadcasted by TVB2 (TV Beograd), or 'the Second of the Slavs' as people used to call that channel.' We used to gather and watch the serial secretly.

Indeed, 'The Sportive Rubrique' was enriched, especially when they started broadcasting the handball games of men and women.

It was proposed that the Rubrique would go live and also involve an auditorium and a performing team. In those days the Variety Show of Vlora was part of the programme too. This continued for a while, until Ladi was summoned and told that he had to leave the programme. He was considered to be cold and not communicative enough. He got sad and somehow disillusioned because he had invested a lot of energy in the programme and had closely cooperated with two directors Albert Minga and Osman Mula. He did not go on TV or on stage for nearly four years after that. Later, by order of the General Director of RTSh, he was invited back to the programme.

The Albanian television covered everything that happened in the country, in sport and other areas, but always within the framework of controlled propaganda. The broadcasting of the World Championships and Olympic Games started in the 80s. In 1985-86 they started live broadcasts, and the TV sports team was expanded, as Ladi could not handle all of it by himself.

Ladi had travelled abroad relatively 'early'. The definition of 'early' makes sense if we consider this in relation to the exodus of the Albanians in the beginning of the nineties, and their continuous ongoing migration. So 'early' for us who lived under the communist regime was the sixties, the 1970s, and the eighties. Earlier than those decades, would put Ladi among the generation of Albanian students who studied in the Soviet Union and were distinguished for their good education and culture, and the simple fact that Moscow had opened their eyes. Vladimir Grillo did not belong to this generation of nostalgic Russophiles; he was born at the end of the Second World War and was brought up in socialist Albania.

One cold evening, in early November, in the beginning of the 90s, Ladi was walking slowly together with some friends and was looking with curiosity at the windows of the red light district in Brussels. From a half-open door, a petite woman showed her laced black tights and called out to Ladi.

For my compatriots, one of the peculiarities of the Low Countries is the legalisation of prostitution. And indeed this girl with her laced black tights and a red bra did not look scared at all. She was amused by the stupor of Ladi and his friends and called out to him once again: 'O Ladi, O Lad Grillo!' She, like many of us who grew up under the dictatorship, considered Ladi Grillo familiar. Indeed, in a closed Albania of that time, Ladi was well-known. He was a sport commentator for more than three decades at the only television station in the country. So he was recognised on the streets of Belgium by an Albanian citizen who was now working as a prostitute there.

In the big world, the Albanians who got out of the darkness resembled the provincial characters of O. Henry when they reached the American metropolitan in the beginning of the twentieth century. With no real sense of direction, lost in translation and afraid about the fatal consequences of a single step. The people working at the Albanian Radio Television in the 80s recall a meeting with the party organisation, which 'debated' penitentiary measures to be taken against two engineers who had worked with RTSh. These two engineers were to be punished simply because they had gone to see a movie with 'sex scenes' while abroad. They were later also denounced by their colleagues at RTSh.

During the last years of transition, Ladi had also worked as a commentator on another specialised sport channel, so that he could make ends meet. But unlike many of his colleagues, even after the country opened up and several private television stations were established he continued to work at the RTSh. For forty-three years he had shared his opinions and emotions through the TV screen about all kinds of sports. To me – and not only to me – Ladi had often appeared somehow 'cold' or, better said, 'reserved' like a Buddhist monk. But it's precisely these qualities and his tranquil and controlled manner of commenting which had made him so agreeable and so acceptable.

Now after all these years of work he has retired. Like everyone who works for many years in the same enterprise and the same profession, Ladi still continues to live with and to think about sport. The milestones of the coming months and years are still the big sports events – the Olympic Games, the championships, the cups. But being free has its advantages as well. Ladi has time to enjoy, to reflect and to tell us about the past. Here is how our conversation went:

Many people know me and greet me in the street, and some even joke about the shortcomings in my commenting of several years ago, but most of the people are friendly and value my opinion. I'm often still invited as a 'guest in the studio' to comment on sports events. Before the nineties, it was difficult (or rather we were not allowed) to show our emotions, and outbursts on the TV were prohibited, despite my nature. It was difficult to be yourself in the years of the dictatorship. That is how it was. But after the nineties we are all somewhat freer and I'm not the 'cold-blooded' commentator anymore.

My work received my undivided passion. I've seen and commented on various sport disciplines and the emotions and pleasure I got from this work have been extraordinary.

It is not a good thing to be a fan. I prefer to use the Albanian expression 'sport lover'. Maybe I've been inclined to support the Partizani team. They used to practice at the 'aviation' field. As a child, I hung out there with my friends. So it's nostalgic for me, as it brings back childhood memories. Certainly during my career, I've faced pressure to report in favour of one or another team, but in general I tried to be neutral and not support a side.

I'm fond of individual sports, such as athletics, swimming, synchronised swimming and artistic skating. But certainly, a beautiful goal remains beautiful. The strong disciplines bring strong emotions. A football match remains a battle to become a winner within a specified time. For example, I will always remember Kushta's goal in Belgrade in 1987. 'Flamurtari' of Vlora was playing against 'Partizan' of Belgrade. It was decided that the Albanian television would broadcast the match live. The Albanian delegation was very well received. When Kushta scored, I lost my breath and my voice, and could hardly report for a while because of the emotion. Magical moments. Then I burst out 'Goooooal!' I was crying. It was a qualifying goal. The match ended 2-1 for the Yugoslavs but we qualified because we had already won 2-0 in Albania. 'Partizan' of Belgrade was a very well-known team then. After the match, the radio commentator from Prishtina told me that the Yugoslav commentator had put it very nicely: 'Kushta sent the ball where the spider makes its nest'. I went and met the Yugoslav commentator thereafter, and thanked him for his beautiful words. It was indeed an unforgettable day.

Our return after that match was painful. In Shtoi farm and in Shkoder they had arranged for a welcoming banquet. But we were held for several hours at the border at Hani i Hotit. Customs confiscated a few things that the footballers had managed to buy while in Belgrade, like clothes and small TV sets. We all got tense and desperate. The magic of the victory was overshadowed by all of this.

If I had the opportunity to start once again, no doubt I would go again for sport. Sport encourages you to enjoy every moment of life, because it's all unrepeatable. Tonight Kukes football team plays in Sarajevo. So far Kukes has done well. Of course I'm keen to know how it will go there. My father's desire was to see me working with language as well as journalism. He agreed to journalism, but did not like the sports direction. He thought I would continue in the family tradition. But our family has been connected with sport journalism for many years now. Kristofor Grillo used to be the editor of the newspaper *Popular Sport*. My cousin Kosta Grillo has become a good sports commentator. In short it's a choice I don't regret.

I remember when I started as a commentator, we used to broadcast among the people in the stadium; a man lit a cigarette, brought it to me and said, 'Take it son, you are working hard'. I considered working at the Albanian television, a serious occupation, dignifying and with continuity. It was probably not the best paying job, but I still enjoyed working there. RTSh still has the rights to broadcast the Olympics Games, the championships and the European football championships. RTSh has always given a lot of attention to sports. During my career I've commented on TV for the last seven Olympic Games. Perhaps this is a record to remember.

Being a sports journalist, I had the opportunity to grow in my profession, to experience incredible emotions and gain knowledge, insight and experience in the world. In 1991 I went to Greece for the Mediterranean Games. Formally I was not obliged to report about the lives of immigrants there. But it was the year when Albania opened up. I was very happy that I was able to travel abroad on duty, but I could not ignore the fact that the roads were full of Albanian immigrants. They had passed through customs, many were on foot, the only thing they wanted was to flee. How many of them have disappeared without a sign!? During those days, our crew interviewed many immigrants and the interviews were broadcast at RTSh.

I felt very good abroad. I'm proud to be Albanian. Wherever I've worked I felt respected. My colleagues around the world also appreciated the fact that I was dedicated to sports. And I've visited many countries and places where Albanian sportsmen were presented, among them Russia, Tunisia, Norway, The Netherlands, Belgium, Australia, Georgia, Turkey, Bulgaria. During these trips I brushed up my Russian and started speaking English.

I would say sport encourages and fuels patriotism. For example, our victory in Belgrade which I just spoke of, or the Albanian Euro 2016 team, made me feel proud. I think people experience the same emotions when they see or hear about their compatriots achieving in other areas of life like art and science as well. That is why we should not hold sport responsible for fuelling nationalism. Certainly, television broadcasting of football matches mobilises people massively. Nevertheless, I had tried to bring out pure emotions for the sport, rather than attempting to manipulate the feelings of the sport lovers to be nationalistic.

Politicians try to politicise sports. In the isolated and closed Albania, all the achievements of the capitalist world were denied or ignored. But I tried not to politicise my commenting. I tried to give the most beautiful moments, to keep it all acceptable and share the most powerful emotions, often amid debate and tension. My concern was to share an emotion, a sports event, even if the United States or the Soviet Union won the first places, and the medals. I think we have to understand and recognise that there is no sport without investment. Passion alone is not enough.

I recall one trip to Tunisia. From the hotel balcony we could watch the tartan runway where young pupils were training. In Albania, until now, we still have no tartan track. I think as long as there are no serious investments in sport, one should not expect more from our athletes and sportsmen in general.

Nowadays the funding comes from the state, as well as from the private sector. The private sector is primarily keen on football, because they see the profit opportunities there. In my opinion, this is wrong, as I think we need investment in individual sports as well. Albania could also do very well with talented individuals. There are talented Albanian sportsmen, especially in the heavy sports like weightlifting and wrestling. Here and there you would also find talented athletes and chess players.

I also recall the two Albanian sportsmen, Pirro Dhima and Luan Shabani, both nineteen years old, when they became 'sports masters'. They were gifted and though very young became champions in Albania and the region. But we did not know how to keep them. As soon as the country opened up, they went to Greece. It was 1991. The Greeks had seen them during the regional championships. They offered

Dhima and Shabani the opportunity to develop and to benefit from their talent. Since then both represented Greece internationally and have won many Olympic titles.

Our athlete Luiza Gega has performed very well in recent years. Like many other individual sportsmen, she needs support and infrastructure. Erald Dervishi is a grand master in chess. He was coached by Fatos Muça, the first Albanian international master. I've had the great pleasure to see them winning. I also grieve when I see them losing.

The world would have a great void without sports. Sport has been a part of mankind since the birth of civilisations. I remember the poem of Fan Noli: 'Run marathonomak run!' Sport today represents peace and sport means an absence of real war. So sport is the management of the war in a peace situation. It is a duel between those who claim to be equal. However, sport is also affected by other factors such as tradition, physical strength, mental strength and certainly the investments made.

The most beautiful period in my life was when our daughter Dena was born. It was an indescribable joy. Other moments relate to work achievements, like the celebration of my career of 45 years in RTSh. There have been many other family events and social happenings over the years. Finally, today what makes me exceptionally happy is the fact that I've become a grandfather.

The worst period in my life was when I lost my parents. If I go back years in time, a terrible period was the obligatory military service, the so-called *zbor*.

We had to march thousands of kilometres then. It was really strenuous. I also recall trembling with hunger in periods when we got food in rations and had to wake up at 2 am and queue for it.

To tell you the truth, I feel peace when I visit a church. My parents were atheists and my brother and I were brought up as atheists. Still my grandmother always took us to her church in Vuno village. For me it's another experience, another outlook, no more than that.

I can't separate the idea of Albania from Europe. Albania is part of Europe, with all its heritage as well as disadvantages. I feel European as much as I feel Albanian. I hope that one day all Albanians will really feel that they belong in Europe and really feel part of it.

※

I will remember and I will live. My greatest passion has always been traveling with my family, with friends, but also alone. I love the Albanian coast, perhaps because my family comes from there and I've spent my childhood there. When I started working at RTSh, I met Kiço Fotjadhi from Dhërmi. I considered him my mentor, and he did support me. At the same time another interesting and significant TV personality is Dhimitër Gjoka, also from Himara. For many years I've worked together with operator Astrit Omeri. He used to be a mountaineer and a passionate traveller. He possessed a motorcycle and together we have travelled all over the country. I hope to travel and visit New Zealand one day. I went to Australia on the occasion of the Olympic Games, but did not go any further. This will remain a dream.

Life is beautiful and I always felt beauty in writing, in painting, in music, in sports, in every artistic aspect of life. I had different 'heroes' during different stages of my development. In particular, I love and enjoy poetry. Sergei Yesenin, to me, remains unreachable. Remember his poem *Letter to Mother*? It starts with:

> *Still around, old dear? How are you keeping?*
> *I too am around. Hello to you!*
> *May that magic twilight ever be streaming*
> *Over your cottage as it used to do.*

Eda

> *Of all creatures that can feel and think, we women are the worst treated things alive.*
> Euripides, Medea, 431 B.C.

'You have been brought up without the fear of the institution, without the indispensability of parades, without the presence of the monumental, without the need to have two faces, one for the world and one at home. My theory of intervention and the necessity of control crumbles before your joyful and natural 'laissez-faire'. The conditions in which you were brought up changed without causing you so much as a headache; that is why you respond so well to change, why you adapt so easily – as if it were the natural state of things. My fear is this: will you be strong enough to defend yourself when the world turns against you? Is your skin tough enough, burned by a Social Darwinist sun, to survive? And do you really need to be so strong, or am I inventing threats, if only because my youth was so different from yours?'

These lines belong to 'Twice 26', an essay that my friend Eda Derhemi dedicated to her daughter Ada. Eda left Albania when she was 26 years old. On her daughter's 26th birthday, she reflects on the past and on their mother-daughter relationship. It seems as if Eda is trying to compare what is incomparable: the experience, common to many, of living under two different systems in two different countries. She shares this experience with millions of people, with hundreds of thousands of young mothers from Albania and all over the Eastern Bloc who, with the fall of the Iron Curtain, hit the road and emigrated to the West in search of a different and better life. I am sure that all of us who did this experienced intensely the departure, the distance, the return. But what proves difficult, if not impossible, is to share our experience with our children, especially the younger ones who blindly trusted us throughout our adventures. Even today they are unable to grasp our worries, our *doubts, our pain, despite the fact that we left our homeland and emigrated partly to secure their future. Their refusal to hear us, their 'insensibility' or desire to remain impervious to our 'survival' talk is evidence of the fact that they are untouched by it, that they are, in a sense, pure. We may understand from this that the protective walls that we erected about them, often ridiculous and sometimes pathetic, have served their function.*

Eda continues in her letter: 'How different are we, or how similar can we be, when our lives have been shaped by totally irreconcilable cultures? A young man I knew once complained about my generation – who were young in the eighties – saying in essence that we are a sentimental generation, one which has difficulty building a normal relationship with the present, or indeed the future, a generation that was not successful during the Socialist period and is not today. I do not believe that generations are characterised by fundamentally different features, but impactful events can leave visible marks on a whole generation. I believe my generation may be sentimental, but I do not see this as a negative trait. Another characteristic of my generation, I think, is our unquestioning attitude to work: Work makes the man, whether you like it or not and independent of any value you attach to it. This remains an instinctive, irreversible and not easily explicable aspect of our lives. I consider this a healthy gene that I can pass on to you. I've often told you that many things I had to learn in the past, things which seemed useless at the time, have proven useful to me later in life. I have not insisted that you trust me on this, because at a certain age it sounds absurd, I know, but I kept telling you, as often as I could, because I am a zealous behaviourist.

I want to believe that there is no alternative to hard work, to working obsessively, and that work has a value in and of itself. When I was 26, my world was harsh and my homeland was made of stone. That is what made me what I am. But I am not sure this is the best way of being. Luckily, your 26 years have been different. You do everything with ease, without so much pressure and with-

out the dilemmas that loomed so large for me. And you smile, more than I ever did. You are peaceful, whereas I was a fighter.... I fight hard for everything because I have to earn it if I am to love it.'

Eda's writing pains me, even though I might think differently; firstly, because we belong to the same generation and have followed the same path and, secondly, because Eda's mastery of the Albanian language makes me feel like a student.

Eda has lived and worked for many years in the United States of America, but she remains deeply engaged with Albania and the Balkans. She does not avoid debate. Her writings are published online, as well as in several serious Albanian newspapers and magazines. They explore diverse social, cultural and political problems besetting Albanian society in both a regional and a global context. More than anything else her writing breathes freedom and emancipation. She has this to say about being free and different in her childhood, in her youth and today:

Forty years ago, in 1975, I was a pupil at the elementary 'Red School' in Tirana. I was a good pupil and a devoted pioneer, but I was uncertain about myself and had many fears. I was the commander of the pupils' league. I recited, took part in competitions, liked to dress well, despite how little we had then. I was a teacher's daughter and that meant something. At home they used to speak very badly about Enver Hoxha. I knew the world was complex. I understood this better than my friends. I had survived some difficult times, things the other children did not know about and would never have to go through. I understood the adults around me and I believe I was very sensitive for my age. This was perhaps my outstanding character trait.

In 1995, two decades ago, I was 32 years old. I had applied for a Master's program at an American university. I lived in Sicily together with my daughter Ada, who was 7 years old. I adored Sicily, but I didn't want to live there. I had many friends, but I was not proud of anything. I worked at three or four jobs at the same time. I wanted my daughter to have the best possible life. I was alone. I was not divorced, but separated from Ada's father. I had lovers, but I didn't want to join forces with any of them. In brief, I didn't know where I was. I was lost. And all this after a good start in Albania, lecturing at Tirana University between 1990 and 1994, and working on my PhD thesis. My life and the life of many others who, like me, abandoned the straight career path laid out in front of us became problematic. Not because of the experiences we had, but in terms of handling practical life and the material consequences of our choice.

Nowadays I have a mind of my own. Here at home, at the university, in the neighbourhood as well as with friends, people know that I'm quite atypical of my community. And they often tell me that I'm crazy. For me it's enough that they let me be myself and love me.

I believe I've always been free, even in the days of communism, when I trembled with fear thinking that maybe I had said something that I shouldn't have. I was brought up in a family that was fundamentally anti-communist, and I believe that made me freer than others. But I also suffered more than the rest. When I was born, my great-grandfather told my parents that they were wrong in giving me a name without meaning: Eda. He decided that for my family, at home, in the neighbourhood and among relatives, I would be 'Elira' which means 'to be free'. Maybe it was he who inspired in me the desire to be free, to have an independent mind and to strive to know myself better.

Eda and I met and re-discovered each other after many years apart, during a trip to Kosovo. As it happens with those who believe in miracles, as soon as we had exchanged a few words, we felt affection for each other once again and took great pleasure in each other's company for the next few days. I remember the bonding happened in a few moments as the Tirana airport bus slowly crossed the hundred meters of the taxiway to bring us to the plane. Spending time with Eda in Prishtina and meeting my friends Nora, Astrit and Blerim there was a real feast. Wherever Eda is today, I feel her intensely. The time span between our meetings is filled with poetry, writings and impressions, photographs, recipes, mutual affection and understanding.

It might well be that the period in which we grew up, made of friendship, is an indispensable institution. I continue to relate to people intensively. I have friends all over the world, but my Mediterranean friends are the best I have. I have many American friends. We get along very well, but I don't stick fast to them the way I do with my old friends. Friends have a special place in my heart and I act without thinking too much in relation to them. Certainly my ideas about friendship were forged during my early youth, and contain romantic, folkloric, even religious, elements. My idea of a friend is almost chivalric, but I don't think that's a bad thing.

I see identity as the most complex and fluid thing about an individual, particularly in relation to the kinds of days, events, friends we experience, the places and times we live in, as well as the physical and psychological features of an individual. All these – as well as the things with which we identify or are proud of (for example an affinity with literature or art during childhood), even the features and tendencies we might not want to talk about, such as material greed, childhood traumas or odd coincidences – make us the way we are, unique and incomparable in our identity. This is the only thing an individual leaves behind in terms of memories or influence. I was close to my grandmother during my childhood and it has affected me more than I could have imagined. As time goes on I feel how strongly she is present in me.

It doesn't seem to me to be a coincidence that all my girlfriends in this book, Albina, Eda and Iris, more or less of the same age, know how to live and enjoy life intensely, whereas I'm usually affected by important events only indirectly, and I often catch myself daydreaming and red-handed in another reality. Because I'm conscious of my lack of direct response to my surroundings, I try to find friends as grounded and vigilant as possible. Eda continues:

Perhaps my strongest characteristic is my capacity to give myself totally to what I'm doing, whether it's dancing, swimming, falling in love, studying for an exam, running, or cooking a tagine chicken. I'm totally involved in what I'm doing and I would advise anyone not to get in my way because I can be very rude. I don't think this has anything to do with my education, my upbringing or any rationalising on my part. Simply put, it's my 'ego' which, according to Jung, is in a dynamic relationship with my 'self'. The relationship between the two is a constant challenge. To my surprise I often find my ego willing to checkmate myself – a good excuse for a glass of wine.

❖

I love people and I've been lucky enough to know many wonderful people. When I hear people say that humans are bad, I really have no idea what are they talking about. Certainly, in the political sense of the word, the world is full of injustice. My world was harsh, but it was fantastic.

What I consider important is being able to keep one's dignity. It has extraordinary value for me. That is why when I'm mistaken or in the wrong I apologise, because in that way I hold on to my dignity and can still be myself. I'm very enthusiastic, sometimes more than I should be, but the principle 'treat others as you would be treated' (independent of who he or she is) saves me a lot of trouble and gives me confidence. All the people I love are very important to me, particularly my daughters. I would like to share with them all the good things I've achieved in life, as well as explain all the bad or stupid things that I've done as well. This matters to me. I don't believe in writing for posterity, which is why I don't write as much as I should and as much as others expect of me. I believe what we leave to our children, friends, colleagues and relatives is a legacy of memories and the legacy of our example.

I'm really very fond of my family. I love them and I take care of them. My husband tells me I behave like a mother to all of them. Perhaps it's true. I cook a good deal, I clean, I restore order to the house, I tell them how and what they should eat, I don't let them drink soft drinks with added sugar, I urge them to read and I want to kiss and hug them nonstop. This might have to do with our family tradition; people were so close in my family, maybe more than we should have been and in a way that was somehow abusive. But my husband and my daughter love my 'abuse' of them and when they complain it's with love.

My ideal as a woman would be to bear children forever, independent of my age and with all the men I've truly loved. This would have made me happy. But I've experienced happiness and I don't have regrets. Giving birth is a sacred act and I bow to every stage of procreation, from the moment when you are on fire with desire to have a child with the man you love, to the moment when you scream at your daughter about her clothes, which need to be put in order before the guests arrive.

I feel fundamentally, totally, internally and formally Albanian. And at the same time I feel American, Italian, French, German... and if I were allowed by other nationalities to claim them too, I would like to feel as much African, Australian, Asian, etc. But if I could choose one country amongst them all, and be a product of that country, Albania would fulfil that function very well. I don't agree with the idea that there are countries where one can't live. People always find a way to live until they are totally oppressed. The nature of freedom differs from one place to another. And even if you are not oppressed, you will still die one day.

So I feel fine wherever I am. I like the big city beat very much, whether I'm wandering aimlessly or have a to-do-list with seventeen activities in a day. But I also like areas without any tourist attractions. I believe you get to know the world and its different peoples better off the beaten path. You can't be a global citizen without being a villager. When I come to Albania I travel a lot, especially in the villages. I say 'come to' Albania, which suggests I always feel as if I'm partly there. Wherever I am, I need to have a physical relationship with the earth, the mud. I love my garden, my flowers, my herbs and my vine.

In my dreams I live on top of a mountain, looking out towards the sea but not too close to it. I don't need a luxurious villa; I want a little house with a lot of light, about twenty minutes away from a village and one hour away from town. I would like to have water and the internet in this place. Actually I would prefer to grow old working in Albania or Sicily. I would play host to a lot of friends in my house. This is my dream for my old age but... everything in its time, because I'm still young.

It might be a good idea to pause and ponder on the verb 'to come' that Eda uses to describe her returning to Albania. I think this verb, this way of thinking about is the foundation of the relationship that many emigrants have with their homeland. I often use it too. I read it and I hear it articulated by other friends who do not live in their birthplace, but refer to their return to their homeland as 'coming' and not 'going'. As if we are spectators on one side of the border, at the gate as it were, looking at ourselves descending the stairs of the airplane or off a boat, loaded with presents and ornaments, holding the hands of bilingual children, somehow careful, somewhat anxious, feeling acutely every single step we take, unsure how to express the joy and the homesickness we feel on both sides of the border as we greet ourselves. The verb 'to come' is there to make sure we connect with ourselves which are split in two. There is a beautiful, painful Albanian expression which has a kind of truth for me: 'The stone is heavier in its place'. I say this, aware of the fact that all 'the stones' that have changed place, willingly or unwillingly, often redefine or enrich the meaning of place and of the world too. Perhaps that is why Eda writes to her daughter in this way:

'There is one angle from which I can look at you with ease: you are free psychologically and physically to go for what you want, to pursue your studies, to deconstruct and reconstruct your life, not because there is no alternative but because there are many alternatives, all tempting and there for the taking. I was not free to choose when I was 26 years old and most people of your generation in Tirana are still not free. Their parents – my generation – still try hard to keep their heads above water, to bring the next generation to dry land. When I think of them, when I see how parents in Albania try so hard to clear a path for their children, to ensure that they study abroad, to create a space that is still denied to the youth of Albania, I'm less worried about you. I feel then that our emigration has brought about one good thing at least. I remember a radical feminist who told a group of contemporary feminists: 'We fought so that today you can use Botox'. And I smile. And I want you to smile, knowing that you have your freedom, you have the miracle of yourself, and you just have to learn how to give it to the world... for the 260 years to come.'

I relate literature and teaching in a rather complex way. Growing up in Albania, we read everything 'good' that was published at the time. We had to. We felt compelled to be aware, to absorb everything that was produced. In that sense my life has changed a good deal. Firstly, the good things do not come in drops as they did when we lived in Albania; secondly, I would have no time for work if I read everything and followed all the cultural activities that I'm drawn to. Teaching is tough and time consuming. Researching a literary subject necessarily focuses you on a special area of interest and you have to concentrate on that, which leaves no time to read everything else. I believe in the value of reading and not just to relax but I have so little time and I want to do so much. I want to write. I still do not write regularly. I work, I follow the news and I devote less time to literature and the arts these days. I tell myself that when I retire I will be able to do the things that I can't do now, but it's possible I'm deceiving myself.

I'm very fond of America and of my husband. Jerry is not a typical American. He is honest, simple and direct like many Americans of the Midwest and I like those qualities. He is very bright and has a perfect instinct for language. He has studied 15 languages and reads everything that is written. As a linguist he analyses words and texts and builds up jokes with 20 linguistic layers. Unlike the typical American, he likes to travel, he is very critical of his own country and is a natural leftist. He has some 'secret' qualities that have made me stay with him for the past twenty years. He has a good soul and still knows how to weave dreams despite growing old. He loves me enough to indulge my eccentricities and he makes me laugh. One thing that distinguishes him from most Albanian men is that he expresses his feelings very well, including his love for me. He tells me in words, in long clear letters, in poems, that he loves me. I have loved other wonderful men who didn't have his ability. I reject the idea that men are allowed to feel but are not allowed to tell you how they feel, that this is what is expected from a man. I feel hurt if you don't tell me how and what you feel for me. Maybe this is very personal but I'm very open in my feelings towards others and I expect the same from them. In brief, I need a man who uses his mouth and my husband fulfils this need.

For me, the word is *life*: I chew it, I analyse it, bend it, create it, squeeze it, kiss it, fall in love with it. I live it and make it and it hurts me, but I'm afraid to translate it. The word is my master. I don't have a profession other than teaching but if there is anything scientific in what I do, it relates to linguistics. When people ask me what my profession is, I normally say either teacher or linguist because my research field is sociolinguistics. Studying languages has made me very sensitive to words. Sometime I see more than is necessary in a word. Close friends and smart people of my acquaintance have told me that I over-analyse a text – a professional liability perhaps, but one which I appreciate more than not being able to draw out the linguistic, political and cultural inferences in a text. After all, it's my job to analyse the text, to be linguistically aware, and I do this with pleasure.

My grandmother on my father's side passed away when I was 23 years old, but I still feel her presence all the time. I don't resemble her but every day she is brought to life through memories, words and smells. She is the one person I have really missed in my adult life. I miss all that she means to me – her ladylike manners, her tenderness, sweetness, humility, obedience, her dedicated service to others, her heart, her sacrifice – no single quality, but all of her qualities together. My grandmother was not educated, and she did not enjoy what I call freedom – she totally lacked a capacity for rebellion so in that sense she is the opposite of the woman I aspire to be – and yet I've not thought so intensely about any other person in my life.

My new family in America and my family in Albania are both essential to me. Some teachers at college have been also special. The endless sacrifices that my mother and father made were fundamental to the freedom – and everything else – I enjoyed when I was young. My life as a girl was completely free of the obligations that other Albanian girls were expected to fulfil. Our parents took care of everything for us so we would have time for school and for cultural activities.

My daughters have kept me busy and may have given me sleepless nights but more than this they have given me much joy. My husband has fulfilled my dreams and wishes, and has also made me feel free by helping me keep true to myself.

My dreams have changed with time. I don't dream now of going abroad; that was a dream belonging to my youth. I would have liked very much to become a film director. Maybe I will go to film school once I retire. I would like to study film directing. I love films because my father was a cameraman. I have an affinity with the camera, and am drawn to the dreams that are woven in this fantastic dimension – symbolic lives as timeless as the language itself.

I was always afraid of the other – of the *Sigurimi*, of the state, the police – day and night. This may have resulted from the way we used to live and think differently at home compared with our public selves. This was a fundamental contradiction with the regime. In those days I could not understand why we were so 'against'. I lacked the philosophical understanding and this added to my fear. In my fear I even had to forget that I was afraid, that I had to live a double life, just so I could manage to live one way of life at a time. All in all, I had a good life. I was surrounded by love, I had many friends, my life was full, we went on holiday and enjoyed some degree of variety. If I describe what in those days I considered variety to my daughters they would not agree with me, but it's all relative. What is important is how you experience life. I still live in opposition to the communist regime. I never loved that regime, I'm grateful for nothing and can't find anything positive to say about it, nor am I able to justify it. I find it absurd when people say: 'Indeed it was a totalitarian regime, it murdered and punished people simply for disagreeing with it, for being free, but it also did some good things – it eradicated illiteracy, it strengthened the schools...'. For me this is either hypocrisy or incomprehension.

I have had many bad days and difficult months, but no bad times. I love my bad days, even my worst ones. I have learned a lot from them, even though I've sometimes felt sad. I have often been alone. I have been afraid. I believe I've confronted the fundamental fears that life gives rise to. Perhaps dealing with death is the remaining challenge for me. I feel as if I'm at peace with death but I'm not sure. I fear its infinity. Infinity scares me. But then again, I can't really talk about having a pact with death so long as I'm healthy. You can't really know how brave or rational you are until you meet death head-on.

I lived 26 years in Albania, 5 years in Italy, and have now lived 21 years in America. I live life intensely, giving and taking as much as possible with the people around me, and I feel that my experiences in the three countries have the same value. I feel very much at ease in all three, I feel at home. I love them and I'm also critical of them, as I am of people dear to me, people who understand me and accept me. Although I live far away, I remain at heart Albanian. I probably write more about Albania than about anything else. Albania moves me and disturbs me profoundly. I don't know why. Perhaps it has to do with the fact that it's where I first learned about the world, my character was moulded there, and in a way these things are connected.

 I would love Albania to be a place where honest people and professionals choose to build their lives without dreaming of going somewhere else. I would love an Albania without corruption, where the nurse and the cook are not unemployed until after they vote for the government; an Albania full of qualified people who, even if they are not the best, still know how to do the job. I long for an Albania characterised by knowledge and dignity.

I have written about my relationship with God. It's complicated. I believe that, during the various phases of our lives, we position ourselves differently in relationship to the Divine, as we try to find a solution to the problems that we face. Given the way our generation was brought up, it's really difficult to be religious. We were moulded in a barren climate in which theological discourse was totally absent. Even when it came to doubting oneself, debating one's deeds, it took place in a vacuum, a culture that was violent towards natural human development. The 1970's were critical for us, decisive in our formation, but that decade is known for its atheistic ideas. However, I think our lack of contact with religion did not harm me much. Everything I know and learn as the days go by makes me even more sure of my inclination to distance myself from religion and not to believe in God unconditionally. Alvin Plantinga, one of the most well-known Christian philosophers within academic circles in America today, thinks that if he had not left Harvard to study philosophy at Calvin College he would not be a Christian today. No doubt, we are affected by our education and our environment but these influences are not necessarily direct.

What disturbs me most is that we Albanians do not meditate as much as we should, we do not question ourselves and our conduct as we should, with regard to the many questions posed by our existence. If we were to consider our relationship with God, outside of a religious framework, it would be energy and time well spent, independent of any result. I'm aware that it's hardly possible to separate God from a religious framework of ideas and to consider a relationship between God and unbelievers is rather utopian, unless we believe in the *sensus divinitas* as Plantinga does, something with which he believes all humans are born. Plantinga considers us atheists as humans with a malfunctioning attribute.

If I were to give you a simple answer to the question about my faith, it would be that I don't believe in God. My daughters are both atheists. They say it's because of me. However, as time goes by, my ideas about God have become garbled and I'm less clear and less firm in my reasoning. My revolutionary soul is flexing. There are moments when I don't want to fight but to rest, and this makes me feel I'm not being myself.

Instead of God, I believe in man. The world is full of wonderful people. I love people very much and I believe in them. Potentially I also believe in damaged people.

My reasoning is not institutional, it's anti-institutional. Europe has an unhealthy, even corrupt, relationship with Christianity. It is actually very problematic and often immoral. I think that both left and right feel ashamed of their history, which is why they do not often discuss their relationship. It is mostly right-wingers who make the connection, though both right and left share this ideology and they both chew on it. The EU's ideals of tolerance and diversity sound empty and hypocritical if we observe the EU's current behaviour in relation to religious issues; for instance, the unjust discrimination against Turkey on religious grounds, or the cultural Islamophobia of EU citizens. I would prefer to see these ideals, not as hypocritical notions but as pillars which support and connect us, and I wish the conservative mentality of European politicians, the men and women who consider the ideological future of the EU, could be persuaded to see them in the same way.

Europeans are ignorant when they consider Albanians to be the ultimate Muslims, or when they consider us to be visionaries and a model for a harmonious future. It bothers me. When people tell me that the majority of Albanians are Muslim, I say 'Yes, I'm one of them' and then I see them rolling their eyes in confusion because this kind of conversation takes place after the third glass of wine. I don't believe in selling our inter-religious peace as a model, because it was created by conditions which are unreproducible by other countries. I believe Albanians should be left to relate to religion however they want to go about it, given their bad record of abuse of individual freedoms under the communists. I would not change one single hair in order to be part of the European Union. I would refuse to explain it to those who do not understand or do not want to discuss it with me. It is not their business. The religion of Albanians has little to do with their acceptance in the EU.

I'd describe a normal day as a day without too much stress. I wake up with a cup of coffee preferably made by Jerry: one shot of espresso with some milk. I take my coffee either talking with Jerry, or reading, or looking at what is happening beyond my windows, amongst the trees there in my garden. I remain quiet and with no special activity for around fifteen minutes. Then I prepare lunch for my youngest daughter Lara, which includes some quick cooking. And I prepare my lectures for the university. I take a bath and I go to work. I spend only two to three hours in my office at the university apart from my teaching hours. I don't like either my office, or the library. I prefer to work at home or at a café and I've been lucky so far in that my job is flexible. Lunch doesn't matter to me. If I'm at home I have a good mixed salad, with lots of cheese, vegetables and fruits. Then I'm busy with my daughter who usually has several extra-curricular activities. Then I work again or I go shopping with Jerry. When Jerry cooks it's a lengthy and elaborate process, so I work and drink some wine while he is busy. Then we go and fetch Lara from her ballet classes and the three of us have dinner together, at least when she is not too late. We have dinner around 7.30 pm which is earlier than the Southern European tradition. I usually drink red wine in the evening. And I work again. If Jerry has found a good movie (from a country or region I know little about), we sit and watch a movie together. I watch TV for nearly two hours every three days. I go to sleep late, sleeping too little and not well. I carry on working or reading in bed until I fall asleep. The most I sleep is six hours a night. I'm a light sleeper. I wake up several times a night and check my email. I'm inclined to answer every single message the moment I see it. I'm not fond of social media and I don't use it to express an opinion or mobilise politically or socially. I read little fiction but I read a lot of scientific literature, which gives me a utilitarian satisfaction, even if superficial. I talk on Skype with my parents in Tirana almost every day and I talk once or twice a day with my older daughter Ada who now lives in Chicago. In spring, summer and autumn I spend a lot of time gardening, looking after the flowers and the vineyard that I've planted.

If I had to leave something for the readers of this book, I'd like to share a few movies that have touched and influenced me, and which I wouldn't mind seeing again and again: Vittorio De Sica's *Bicycle Thieves*, from 1948, Roberto Rossellini's *Rome, Open City*, from 1995, Pier Paolo Pasolini's *Mamma Roma*, from 1962, Federico Fellini's Amarcord, from 1973, and Milos Forman's *One Flew Over the Cuckoo's Nest*, from 1975. I love them because they all show the violent tension that exists between humanity and freedom as unquenchable ideals of the individual and the deep abyss into which humans can fall when they live in deformed moral and political systems.

The absent one

> *Pretty soon, I'll be decomposing into phosphorous, calcium, and so on. Who else will you find to tell you the truth? All that's left are the archives. Pieces of paper. And the truth is... I worked at an archive myself, I can tell you first hand: paper lies even more than people do.*
> Svetlana Alexievich: *Secondhand time. The Last of the Soviets*

'The absent one' is the one who dares to challenge, to go against the stream, by openly thinking and acting differently. The one who was almost captured in a bronze monument. The hero and antihero in one.

This chapter is dedicated to Tefa, Tefalin Malshyti, my university friend. We met for the last time in the summer of 1995. It was mid-July, and I was returning home after six months of study in The Hague. I took a long route, simply because I really did not know if I really wanted to get back to Tirana. We met on the deck of the ship that connected Bari with Durres. We had not seen each other for some years and we had not said farewell or goodbye because Tefa had done something that many Albanians dreamed about, but would not dare to do. He had tried to escape.

Very few people were visiting or returning to Albania on that hot July day. On the deck were two Italian carabinieri. They were accompanying some Albanian girls, who we soon learned were detained and expelled from Italy because of prostitution. They were being delivered back to their home country. The policemen and the girls were quite noisy, talking to each other in loud voices, as if they knew each other from long ago. We were traveling by day, the sun was shining bright, the sea breeze was relaxing and amid that absurd joy, which seemed to be a remnant of the past night, it felt as if there was no place for contemplation or sadness.

Tefa was the first of my friends who was confronted with the border, the state, the court, the prison. He attempted to flee to Yugoslavia, swimming across the Shkodra Lake on June 12, 1989. Shkodra Lake in spite of its beauty and its strategic positioning has taken *the life of many people. As much as it was invitingly warm and not icy cold like Ohrid Lake, it could not be trusted. As a child, I had spent many summer days by the lake, where together with my cousins, we would bike to and from the city. I really used to enjoy spending the summer vacations in Shkodra, with the evening walks in the piazza and swimming in the lake.*

I got to know Tefa when we started university. He was one of the most handsome, well-behaved and smart guys of our group of faculty students. The Shkodra dialect made him pleasantly acceptable in conversation. We had done our first three years and were ready to go to the fourth and final year there.

The news about his capture while trying to flee the country was unexpected. He was one of us, and though many of us entertained the idea of escaping the country, we seldom dared to share these thoughts with each other, and only a reckless, brave young man like Tefa actually tried to escape. The price of this act was very high. If Tefa, who had had the opportunity to study at the university, was not satisfied, felt limited, isolated, and wanted more how would those who were not granted their right to study feel? Those who personified the class enemy, those condemned to work from morning until the evening in the fields, those who would eat year after year only corn bread, those who produced and bottled the milk but would not be able to drink it? Those who harvested the wheat but would be able to eat it, and those who had no perspective at all in Albania, what would they do?

Only with the dawn of democracy, my generation would get to know, to see, to feel, to talk to and to communicate with these 'enemies' of the 'dictatorship of the proletariat', who paid with their lives or with their freedom just because they spoke their mind and expressed their discontent. Many of them did not survive the system, they were executed or buried alive, sent to prisons or forced labour camps, only because they dared to think and to express their thoughts and ideas. Among those were many women and girls: Musine Kokalari, Marie Tuçi, Drita Çomo and many others. They did not live to see the end of the dictatorship and the historical turn towards democracy.

Let us get back to my friend. Even in the year 1989, when the whole communist block was cracking and shaking, those few Albanians who dared to cross the border were caught, punished or killed on the spot. What made the whole act even more tragically cruel and painful was the treatment and persecution of the family they left behind. One of my acquaintances in Tirana, Andrea O, dared to cross the border, hidden in the luggage compartment of a bus full of Dutch tourists. Andrea used to guide the foreigners who visited Albania in those years and as such he was trusted. Upon his escape, his brother was expelled from university, and his aunts, who had brought him up, both communists, were expelled from the party and sent to a remote village. They had to stay there for many years, sickened and distressed to the extreme, and only when the regime fell could they move.

Today Tefa tells me that when he decided to cross the lake and get on the other side, he started with physical training. His friends were surprised by his zeal to become strong and muscular. He felt the regime was living its last hours, but one could not tell how long the terror and its death throes would last. He had no time to lose. Everything he wanted, everything he dreamed about, desired and wished for was on the other side of the border. What he wanted above all was to be free. 'I decided to leave, convinced that one day I would be there for my family'.

Tefa did not tell anyone of his plan to leave, because he did not want to burden anyone else with the responsibility of this 'crazy' act. Indeed, one of the first questions asked under the threat of a pointed gun, when they caught him was, 'Where are your friends?'

Many of us learned the news of his capture a few days after. Tefa grew in my eyes, he became a hero, and he had surprised me. He had challenged the expression: 'the patient one is the winning one'. The end of the regime was not yet in sight when he was captured, so one wondered what would happen to him? How many years would he have to rot away in a prison? Would they torture him? Would he serve to become 'an example'? Would he break? Would he betray his friends?

Tefa tells me that he was badly treated only on the day he was caught. To a certain extent he was lucky. Not because he had a good lawyer who could advise him, because in those days there were no lawyers defending the so-called 'enemy', but his family left no stone unturned and approached powerful people in Shkodra, and eventually someone had shown mercy.

I ask Tefa, 'Why did you want to leave?' It was a question that I felt needed to be answered . An answer that Tefa had not thought about earlier. 'If I had thought about the possibility of being caught, I would not have dared to run away.' For him there was no return, he could not fail.

'I wanted to live and experience the way the people who run away feel and experience running away. I wanted to feel the way they feel when they see the world beyond the borders, because I want to write about their experience in that world.' This is what Tefa had told the officers on duty when he was caught, and thereafter to the inspector that questioned him during his detention.

'To experience the destiny of the runaways' so that he could write about them? It is clear that he was not sane, because no one would swim across the lake..... only to see what was happening on the other side. Clearly he had behaved like a 'reckless, crazy lunatic'. An intelligent way to avoid punishment and a harsh decision by the court. In autumn 1989, Tefa appeared in court. The waves of the Eastern Bloc earthquake were being felt in Albania too. Two of Tefa's best friends, Bland Ashiku and Roland Sejko, went to follow the court proceedings.

Tefa was declared 'not guilty' but 'crazy'. He had to remain in prison in Tirana, at the confinement place reserved for persons with psychiatric problems. It was a difficult time.

'Everything that had happened had left its traces. But I really do not look back and ponder on it for too long. When I go with my children to Shkodra, we often go down to the lake to swim. I've told them what had happened. One time is enough. Life goes on and we do not have much time to lose.'

When I hear him talking like this, it occurs me he is still the same guy I once knew.

'At the hospital, at least 60% of the prisoners were simulating psychiatric problems. The others were indeed either crazy and or depressed. I've lived very intensively in the psychiatric ward/prison. Among them there were also murderers and criminals. I remember listening from the prison to the roar coming from the main stadium in Tirana, when Al Bano and Romina were giving their concert. Things were changing.'

Indeed, the concert of Al Bano and Romina Powell was historic and resembles the first historic show of the Rolling Stones in Havana, Cuba, in March 2016. If not the biggest ever crowd, Al Bano and Romina met the most enthusiastic and enraptured one in Tirana. The Albanians had never seen them perform live, but we could sing all their songs by heart from beginning to the end.

After some months Tefa got out of prison. The events of July 1990, of people storming the embassies in Tirana, found him in Saranda. 'A lost opportunity,' he says. He inquired about the possibility to continue his studies. The Minister of Education granted him the right to continue. Tefa had killed fear. In the autumn of 1990, Ismail Kadare, the internationally well-known Albanian writer, requested political asylum in France. In December, students started protesting, first demanding better living conditions – electricity, heating and better food in the canteen – and then later political pluralism. Tefa is among the leaders of those demanding students. As such he would be the youngest of the founding members of the Democratic Party (DP). Tefa took part in the meeting arranged with Ramiz Alia, and presented the programme with the students' demands, including the demand for political pluralism; in other words, not only demands that dealt with the improvement of the conditions of the students.

Tefa described that period and the current times as follows:

No one in the students' group knew and nor perhaps expected such 'bomb': the demand for political pluralism. Neither did Azem (Hajdari[7]) know what I had written in that piece of paper before the meeting. It has often occurred to me that it might well be that the communist leaders wanted exactly this to happen. The ones that joined the movement later did not really represent the students or the people. First of all, they did not have a Western outlook on the world. They joined the struggle because they saw an opportunity, some because they were ordered to do so, and some because they wanted to benefit from the troubled times. Gramoz Pashko was an exception, but he was not powerful. Aleksander Meksi, who was very withdrawn, was an exception too. They were both emancipated and had a Western outlook on the world. As far as the other 'democrats' were concerned, I didn't see any idealism there. In the ranks of those demanding democracy and pluralism were many communists, the ones who had been so close to the 'nomenclature'. The ones who had really suffered were not there. They were afraid.

But how can the communists accept and even propagate Western democracy and that way of life today, if until yesterday they were the ones who had condemned it? That it why I believe that most probably everything was set up on the instruction of the Communist Party for two reasons: In this way the communists could control the course of the 'opponents' and at the same time could tell the conservative party members at the base that the party was forced to change course because it was under pressure. It can well be that these 'moderated' communists were having problems with the most conservative branch.

One day, after the events of December and the founding of the DP, I was in the offices of the new party, when I heard that many people were leaving the country by boats. I decided to leave the country too. I joined the majority of the potential electorate of DP, which did not win the first pluralist elections. I left Albania on board of the iconic ship, Iliria. I will never forget the lights of a chemical complex, near Brindisi, directing us to the coast, and shining upon us like we were never shone upon before.

We were treated so well in Italy, from the very beginning when we went into camps until we were allowed to move and find our own way and make friends. I stayed in the south of Italy from 1991 until 1997. Then I moved to the north, working at a furniture factory, in Pordenone between Venice and Trieste. I still work there. My job and responsibilities at the factory have changed over the years, because the work process and the staff have changed too. Nowadays there is less demand for this kind of furniture.

The south of Italy differs a lot from the north. Italy is big, it starts at the centre of Europe and stretches up to the coast of Africa. Most of the Albanians who came here twenty-five years ago are well integrated. Only a few did not manage to integrate themselves. It is sad to note that the way the Italians received us can't be compared with the way the refugees from Africa are received today.

Shkodër has become my second home. My mother and my relatives still live there. I go to Shkodër on holidays with my family. My children were born in Italy, in freedom. And they are more rebellious than I am. I'm mostly impressed by my daughter who is really free and has a mind of her own. When I go to Albania by car, we go first to Trieste and then go down through Croatia and Montenegro. The moment we enter the former Yugoslavia, I feel I've reached Albania.

I'm concerned because I see that in Albania the old capitalism, without a human face, is being built. Soon the differences between the Albanian capitalism and the Internet economies will be very evident. I think we should be thrifty and not increase the state loan, so we do not burden the future generations to deal with this. Look now at Greece and the problems they are facing there. As they say 'the squash doesn't always float above water'. I also think the businesses that would like to invest in Albania should not only exploit the cheap labour force, but should also leave something good behind, to the benefit of the country.

We are all unique and different. It is the institutions, both in a communist or capitalist system that try to unify us. However, I've always tried to question the ready-made answers, trying to think of my own answers based on my experience and the experience of the others. Sometimes I've found good answers, sometimes not, but they have still been my answers to the challenges of life. Today people in Albania are free to question the old norms and values of life, they are free to express themselves, not being afraid they will end up in prison. Freedom has become 'quotidian', a normal asset closely connected to our concept of life. I often ask myself how did we do without Internet? I believe today the borders are where you want them to be and I try to keep my borders as far as possible.

I used to like Migjeni[8] a lot. He still remains contemporary and actual. It is sad to think that his house-museum in Shkoder doesn't exist any longer! I used to like Ismail Kadare. His writing and his books used to be the window to the big world. And I value Noli[9] for his work and his life. Nowadays I don't read a lot, due to a lack of time and peace of mind. Lately I read a nice book, very elegant while giving three good reasons to live: friendship, love and art.

I don't identify myself with anyone. It would not be wise. Certainly I share thoughts, life experiences, I share ideas with the community around me and so I find friends, the like-minded, in my case that would be my best friend, Ed Simoni.

I remember one day I was in Venice in the company of Bland, Ed Simoni and Land Sejko. We all got together by chance at my place in Pordenone. This mainly thanks to Bland who encouraged us to get together quickly. We met after so many years. Bland came from Tirana, Landi came by train from Rome and when we got together he proposed to us to go to Venice. There another friend of ours, Adrian Paçi, displayed work at an exhibition called, if I remember correctly: 'My country doesn't exist'.

I often think about what was considered 'right' and 'wrong' in those days, and how we were encouraged not to think, not to reflect but follow the crowd. We were so loaded with prejudices about race and ethnicity, and I think in many of us something of that old mentality still lurks.

As we talk, I'm in a park with Amadeus, my youngest son. Nearby there is a well-'preserved' old white man with white moustache with two black children, also well-dressed and well-mannered. One of the children says to the old man 'grandpa'. And indeed I think how unprepared we were concerning to racial integration. In Shkodra, the city I know best of in Albania, the gypsies, the Roma still live in a ghetto.

As to God, many empires didn't need God. I would identify God with nature. It is the nature of things. For me, God doesn't exist the way it's portrayed. We try to make sense of what is happening around us and for that reason we invent a compass.

But God is inside us, it's our quest to be in harmony with nature and the rest of the universe. In this sense I'm not a believer but a naturalist. And there is not much to do but to live life as Kundera says with 'the unbearable lightness of being'. Time is the compass that dominates everything. And religions try to negotiate our relationship with time, but the most they do is create identities, and nothing more than that.

Today science has surpassed religions in an effort to explain and to improve our lives and everything else that matters for our existence.

I was born in Albania and I have been adopted by Italy. For a great part I feel Mediterranean. I love the sun, the sea, good food and a certain comedy a la Italiana that is born out of the 'quotidian', just like in Shkodër.

I've never been totally out of touch with Albania, but each time I go there and stay for two or three weeks, I really feel the need to return here. I have a life here, my children and my job are here, and I like the city and the citizenship here more. If these things would not weigh so much, maybe I would consider returning to Albania one day. I like some things there too, so perhaps I will return and enjoy them once I retire. For the time being, this is far into the future.

Final words

Two opposing thoughts come to my mind as I try to conclude this book.

We live in troubled and complex times, witnessing clashes of trends, cultures, mentalities and civilisations at the local and global level. Our existence as individuals, in different communities and societies is fragile and dependent of the deeds of adventurous/crazy bankers, bloodthirsty militarists, fundamentalists of many colours, secret services, climate change, and founders of social networks that flood the reality and reconstruct our perceptions.

A less fatalistic and more realistic thought is that today's Albanians, including my friends and my generation, wherever we are in the world, have never been better off, more free, more knowledgeable, more emancipated, better connected, more in the light, better seen and understood. Their Albania, independent of its many 'unfinished businesses' and not yet extinct old mentalities, has never been more prosperous, more beautiful, more attractive.

For those who want to know about the follow-up of these stories, I can say that all my friends are doing well. Of course their portraits are of the current time, or for as long as my friends can identify with them. As time goes by, we can all think, talk and choose to see things in a different perspective.

Acknowledgements

Once again I thank my Albanian friends and wish them time to live, to think and to enjoy.

I want to thank some other people too, without whom this book would not have seen the light of publication. To start with my mother and my father for their faith in me; then my companion John for the inspiration, courage and persistence to see me finish what I start; my family's guardian angels Marius and Gary; Bryony for the time dedicated to English-editing; and my friend Daniel for the design work.

My thanks also go to the team of Kulturvermittlung Steiermark who generously hosted me in Graz as writer in residence in the 2015 term.

Notes

[1] The 11th Song Festival was organised and produced by the Albanian Public Radio and Television (RTSh) in December 1972. The organisers were named 'enemies of the people', for plotting against the party by influencing the Albanian youth. Many were arrested, sent to force labour camps and murdered.

[2] During 1996-97, Albania was shaken by the dramatic rise and collapse of several financial pyramid schemes, Relative to the size of the economy, they were of an unprecedented scale. Many Albanians invested and lost their money in the schemes. When the pyramids collapsed, the country descended into anarchy. Around 2,000 people were killed in what resembled a civil war.

[3] Albanian children used to refer to adults as *teta* and *xhaxhi*, which can be translated into English as *aunt* and *uncle*. In those days we would not refer to grownups as *miss* or *mister*.

[4] Ramiz Alia was the second and last leader of communist Albania from 1985 to 1991, a crucial figure in the peaceful political transition of the early nineties.

[5] The Buna river is the natural border between Albania and Montenegro (former Yugoslavia).

[6] 'Each of them adds something new to our blood, / but they kill themselves off in the process, while we, / renewed by them, are the ones to endure / We're full of vices and horrors and whims'.

[7] Azem Hajdari was the leader of the Student Movement of 1990-91 and the first chairman of the Democratic Party. He was assassinated in 1998.

[8] Millosh Gjergj Nikolla was an Albanian poet and writer known under his *nom de plume* Migjeni, He has a strong individual voice of social protest and has always been very appealing to youth.

[9] Theofan Stilian Noli, better known as Fan Noli, was an Albanian writer, scholar, diplomat, politician, historian and founder of the Albanian Orthodox Church, who served as prime minister and regent of Albania during the 1924 June revolution, until the Government was overthrown by Ahmet Zogu.

Contents

Why this book?	7
Albina	13
Andrea	31
Gazi	51
Birds of a feather flock together	65
Greta	71
Blandi	93
Iris	125
Lazri	141
Ladi	157
Eda	173
The absent one	193
Final words	205
Acknowledgements	207

CARABELA

www.ingramcontent.com/pod-product-compliance
Lightning Source LLC
Chambersburg PA
CBHW071115160426
43196CB00013B/2575